ELECTRONIC
MUSIC
PROJECTS

by

R.A. PENFOLD

BERNARD BABANI (publishing) LTD
THE GRAMPIANS
SHEPHERDS BUSH ROAD
LONDON W6 7NF
ENGLAND

I.S.B.N. 0 900162 94 5

First Published — June 1980

Printed and Manufactured in Great Britain by Hunt Barnard Printing Ltd.

CONTENTS

INTRODUCTION

Although one of the more recent branches of amateur electronics, electronic music has now become very popular indeed. There are many electronic projects which fall into this catagory, ranging in complexity from a simple guitar effects unit to a sophisticated organ or synthesiser. The purpose of this book is to provide the constructor with a number of practical circuits for the less complicated items of electronic music equipment, including such things as a fuzz box, a simple organ, various types of sound generator, tremolo generator, reverberation amplifier, metronome, etc. Most aspects of electronic music will be covered in the range of projects, but complex projects go beyond the scope of this publication and are not included.

In general the circuits are not especially critical with regard to the component layout, and it should not be difficult for near beginners, in addition to more advanced constructors, to build most of the projects featured in the following pages.

CHAPTER 1

GUITAR EFFECTS UNITS

Guitar effects units must be amongst the most popular of all electronic projects. All the more common types will be featured here (treble boost, fuzz, waa-waa, and sustain). The subsequent chapter will deal with further effects units that can be used with a guitar, but are often used with organs and other instruments as well (tremolo, phaser, etc.).

Simple Treble Booster

A treble booster or tone booster unit can be used to give an electric guitar a more "brilliant" sound, and is of particular value when used with an instrument which has a dull tone that is lacking in bite. As the name suggests, a treble booster simply boosts higher frequency components in the signal, which will normally be the higher order harmonics.

It is not necessary for a unit of this type to have some specific frequency response, and there is quite a lot of latitude here. Obviously the amount of treble boost applied, the starting frequency, how peaky or flat the response is made, etc. all affect results produced by the unit, but in practice there are a vast range of responses that will give the general effect that is required.

The circuit diagram of the simple treble booster unit is shown in Figure 1. The basis of the unit is the common emitter amplifier based on Tr1. This has R3 as its collector load and base biasing is provided by R6. When S1 is in the open position, emitter resistor R4 is totally unbypassed, and it introduces 100% negative feedback to the amplifier, reducing its gain to almost exactly unity. Under these conditions the input signal is fed straight through the unit virtually unaltered, and the treble boost effect is switched out.

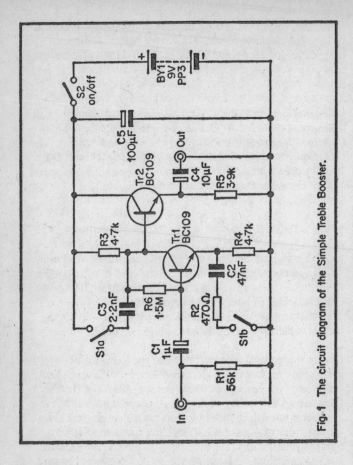

Fig. 1 The circuit diagram of the Simple Treble Booster.

If S1 is closed, C2 and R2 are then shunted across R4. At low
audio frequencies the impedance of C2 is relatively high, and
the gain of the circuit is not significantly altered. However,
at frequencies above about 2 kHz the impedance of C2
significantly shunts R4, reducing the level of feedback and
giving increased gain. R2 limits the level of boost obtained to
a reasonable level.

This simple form of treble boost would give a response that
would rise steadily over a frequency range of about 1 to

4

15 kHz and then flatten out. In units of this type it is normal to tame the response slightly at the very highest audio frequencies and above, for several reasons. Firstly, the output may otherwise sound a little harsh as the very highest harmonics can sound rather unpleasant (they do not actually harmonise with the fundamental frequency). Secondly, untamed treble boost can sometimes result in a rather high background noise level. Thirdly, the boosted response above the audio frequency spectrum could result in increased stray high frequency feedback and consequent instability in the system as a whole.

In this case the response above about 10 kHz is rolled off somewhat by including C3 across collector load resistor R3 when S1 is closed. The impedance of C3 is too high to have any significant affect on the circuit at frequencies below about 10 kHz, but at frequencies above this figure it has a noticeable shunting effect on R3. The gain of the circuit is roughly equal to the collector load impedance divided by the impedance in the emitter circuit. Therefore, the effectively lower impedance of R3 gives reduced gain and the required taming of the upper audio response.

It is necessary for the circuit to feed into a fairly high impedance or loading effects might have a detrimental affect on the response of the unit. A simple emitter follower buffer stage has therefore been included between Tr1 collector and the output socket, and this ensures minimal loading on Tr1 even if the output is fed into a low impedance input. The input impedance to Tr1 is rather higher than is really needed in this application, and, undesirably, varies considerably with changes in the input signal's frequency. R1 is used to shunt the input impedance so as to bring it down to a more satisfactory level of about 40 to 50k. As this resistor largely determines the input impedance of the circuit, variations in the input impedance of Tr1 have relatively little affect on the input impedance of the unit as a whole.

On/off switching is provided by S2 and C5 is merely a supply decoupling capacitor. C1 and C4 provide input and output D.C. blocking respectively. The current consumption of the

5

unit is only about 2 mA., giving very many hours of use from each PP3 size battery.

The frequency response of the prototype unit is shown in Figure 2, and the rising response plus very high frequency taming can both be clearly seen from this.

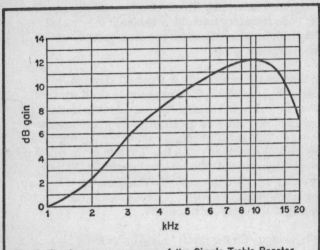

Fig. 2 The frequency response of the Simple Treble Booster.

In use the treble booster should normally be connected between the guitar and the amplifier, although it can handle signals of up to several hundred millivolts R.M.S. without clipping and producing serious distortion, and the unit could be inserted in a higher level signal path if this would be more convenient for some reason. In either case the input and output connecting cables must be screened types. Provided the unit is housed in a metal case which is connected to the negative supply rail there is not need for the leads connecting the circuit board to the input and output sockets to be screened types. Overall screening of the circuit will be provided by the case which will consequently prevent unwanted stray pick-up of signals such as mains hum etc. It is not really advisable to use a non-metallic case for the project as this would leave the unit wide open to stray pick-up. As the unit has only a low voltage gain, and its input and output terminals are out of phase, the layout of the circuit is not at all critical and it is virtually impossible for the unit to become unstable.

Components Simple Treble Booster

Resistors. All ¼ watt 5% (10% over 1M)
R1   56k
R2   470 ohms
R3   4.7k
R4   4.7k
R5   3.9k
R6   1.5M

Capacitors
C1   1 μF 10V
C2   47 nF plastic foil
C3   2.2 nF plastic foil
C4   10 μF 10V
C5   100 μF 10V

Semiconductors
Tr1   BC109
Tr2   BC109

Switches
S1   D.P.S.T. type
S2   S.P.S.T. type

Miscellaneous
Case, PP3 size battery, battery connector, etc. (For the modified version S1 is a 3 way 4 pole rotary type, 2 poles being unused).

Modified Tone Booster

Although the form of treble boost provided by the unit just described is the one most often used, untamed treble boost is sometimes used where a really "sharp" and "bright" sound is required. The circuit of Figure 1 can readily be altered to give switchable tamed and untamed treble boost, the necessary modifications being detailed in Figure 3.

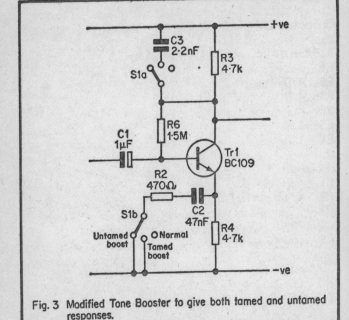

Fig. 3 Modified Tone Booster to give both tamed and untamed responses.

S1 is now a three position switch, the first two positions giving the normal and tamed responses in precisely the same way as the original circuit. In the third position the high frequency roll off capacitor C3 is disconnected from across R3, but R2 and C2 remain shunted across R4. Thus the treble boost is still provided by R2 and C2, but C3 no longer provides any taming of the response, giving the required effect.

The response in the untamed mode differs from that shown in Figure 2 in that it does not start to flatten out somewhat at about 4 or 5 kHz, but continues to rise sharply up to about 10 kHz where there is approximately 18 dB of boost. The response then flattens considerably with the level of boost rising to only about 20 dB at 20 kHz.

Construction of the unit is much the same as for the original version, but good screening is more important due to the increased high frequency gain of the unit. The ideal housing for the unit is a diecast aluminium box, but any all-metal case should suffice.

Fuzz Box

This is another very simple form of effects unit, and is possibly the most popular of all effects units. The purpose of a "fuzz" unit is simply to distort the input signal, usually by clipping it, so as to generate increased harmonic content at the output. This differs from treble boost in that the latter boosts the harmonics generated by the guitar whereas fuzz actually produces new harmonics which are not generated at significant levels by the guitar. Thus the two effects give very different sounds, and are not the same. Furthermore, fuzz also produces intermodulation products and is therefore likely to produce rather unpleasant sounds if more than one note at a time is played. It also gives a sustain effect since the clipping action attenuates the high initial output level from the guitar and boosts the low level signal produced once the signal has decayed. This gives a relatively constant output level and consequently the sustain effect.

The Circuit

The circuit diagram of the fuzz box appears in Figure 4. Most circuits use a high gain amplifier which either clips the signal at its output, or feeds a simple diode clipping circuit. However, this form of circuit does have certain disadvantages, one of which is that the high gain involved makes it difficult to maintain stability. Another is that the high gain can lead to rather a high noise level.

This circuit does not suffer from either of these disadvantages,

9

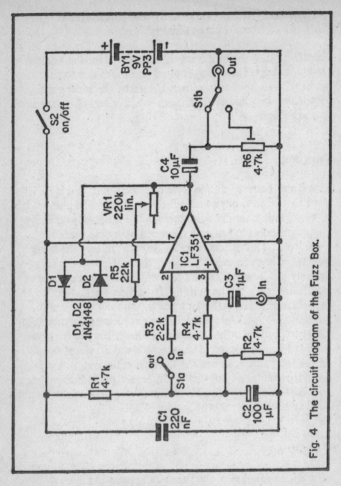

Fig. 4 The circuit diagram of the Fuzz Box.

and uses an operational amplifier clipping circuit. A low noise BIFET type is recommended (e.g. LF351, TL081CP, etc.) since these have a JFET input stage which gives a really low noise level. Very good results should be obtained using an ordinary 741C device though.

Operational amplifier IC1 is used in the non-inverting mode. The non-inverting (+) input is biased to a central tapping on the supply lines by R4. This resistor also sets the input impedance of the unit at the required level of about 47k, the input impedance of the amplifier being equal to the value of this resistor because the f.e.t. input stage of the operational amplifier has an input impedance of many megohms at audio frequencies, and therefore does not significantly affect the input impedance of the circuit. C3 provides D.C. blocking at the input. The central tapping on the earth rail is provided by R1 and R2 with C2 providing decoupling here. Of course, standard operational amplifier circuits use dual supplies, but this method is perfectly satisfactory for a circuit which is only used to handle A.C. signals, and eliminates the need for two batteries.

With S1 in the "out" position, virtually 100% negative feedback is applied to IC1 so that it has a voltage gain of approximately unity. The feedback is applied through VR1 and R5. The signal then passes straight through the unit virtually unaltered, and the fuzz effect is defeated.

The fuzz effect is introduced by switching S1 to the "in" position so that R3 is brought into circuit, and less than 100% negative feedback is applied to IC1. The voltage gain of the circuit is then equal to (R1 + R2)/R1 where R1 is the resistance between the inverting input and the central tapping on the supply, and R2 is the resistance between the inverting input and the output of IC1.

By varying the value of VR1 it will be apparent that the gain of the circuit can be varied from about eleven with VR1 at minimum value up to about 111 times with it at maximum value. However, this is only the case when the output signal level is no more than about 1 volt or so peak to peak. If it should significantly exceed this level D1 will be biased into conduction on positive going output excursions, and D2 will be forward biased on negative output excursions, for the duration that the signal exceeds the forward conduction threshold level.

When the diodes become conductive they greatly reduce the feedback resistance from the output of IC1 to its inverting

11

input, reducing the voltage gain of the circuit to little more than unity. This severely clips the output signal at a little over 1 volt peak to peak, giving the required fuzz effect.

The output from IC1 is too high for most amplifiers, and VR1 can be used to attenuate the signal to the appropriate level. C4 merely provides D.C. blocking at the output of IC1. The depth of the fuzz effect is controlled using VR1. With this set for low gain the output signal level will probably be barely sufficient to cause clipping, giving only a slight effect. Adjusting VR1 for increased gain increases the severity of the clipping and gives a more severe fuzz effect. If the guitar is fitted with a volume control this must be set at or near maximum or the output from the guitar may be insufficient to give the clipping effect.

S2 is the ordinary on/off switch and C1 is a supply decoupling capacitor. The current consumption of the unit is only about 2 mA and the small (PP3 size) battery therefore gives very many hours of use before becoming exhausted.

As with the previous project, it is advisable to house the unit in an earthed metal case such as a diecast aluminium type, so that the circuitry is screened from possible sources of electrical interference. The layout is not too critical despite the fact that the unit has a reasonably high gain and input impedance, and the input and output are in phase. However, care should be taken to ensure that no strong stray feedback path from the output to the input is produced or instability could well result. For example, do not leave long input and output wires trailing around inside the case unless they are screened types. All external connecting cables should of course be screened types so that stray pick up of electrical interference is avoided.

Although the device specified for IC1 has a f.e.t input stage, this is a JFET type and not a MOSFET one. This device (and its equivalents) do not therefore require any special handling precautions as they are not susceptible to damage by high potential static charges.

R1   4.7k
R2   4.7k
R3   2.2k
R4   47k
R5   22k
R6   4.7k 0.1 watt preset
VR1   220k lin. carbon

Capacitors
C1   220 nF plastic foil
C2   100 μF 10V
C3   1 μF 10V
C4   10 μF 10V

Semiconductors
IC1   LF351 or equivalent
D1   1N4148
D2   1N4148

Switches
S1   D.P.D.T. type
S2   S.P.S.T. type

Miscellaneous
Case, PP3 size battery, battery connector, etc.

Waa-Waa Unit

The waa-waa effect is by no means a new one, but has remained quite popular over the years. A waa-waa unit boosts a narrow band of frequencies, and by some means (normally using a pedal) the player varies the boosted band of frequencies up and down over the audio band in a manner that produces the desired effect. This requires a little practice if it is to be done really competently, but is not unduly difficult.

Figure 5 shows the complete circuit diagram of the waa-waa pedal unit. Like the previous circuit, this is based on a low

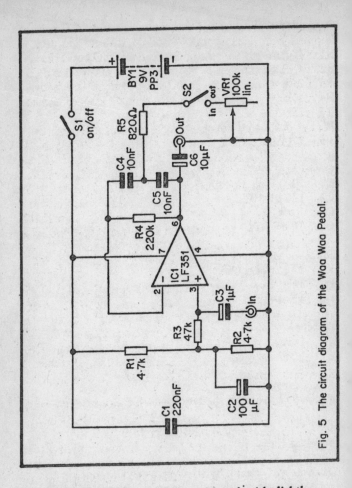

Fig. 5 The circuit diagram of the Waa Waa Pedal.

noise BIFET operational amplifier, although with slightly reduced audio quality an ordinary 741C device can be used. R1, R2 and C2 form a centre tapping on the supply lines and R3 biases the non-inverting (+) input to this. The device is used in the non-inverting mode and so the input signal is coupled to this input by way of D.C. blocking capacitor C3.

R4 provides a D.C. feedback path from the output of IC1 to its inverting (-) input so that the output is biased to the

14

required level of about half the supply potential. A.C. negative feedback is provided through C4 and C5, with R5 and VR1 being used to remove some of this feedback and boost the voltage gain of the circuit. However, the values of C4 and C5 are fairly low, and this results in the very frequency selective feedback that is required to give the peaky frequency response.

For example, at high frequencies the impedance through C4 and C5 is very low, VR1 and R5 then having a relatively high impedance and consequently little effect on the circuit. There is then virtually 100% negative feedback through C4 and C5, giving the circuit a voltage gain of almost exactly unity. At low audio frequencies the impedance of C4 and C5 in series is very high, so that they now have no significant effect on the circuit. Virtually 100% negative feedback is still provided through R4 though, so that the voltage gain of the unit remains at approximately unity.

At middle audio frequencies the impedance ratio of C5 to R5 plus VR1 results in only a modest amount of feedback being applied to IC1, with the voltage gain of the circuit being boosted as a result. There is still a feedback path through R4 of course, but the relatively low impedance path through C4, R5 and VR1 decouples a lot of this feedback, and so it does not greatly restrict the voltage gain of the circuit.

The required peaked response is thus produced, and the centre frequency of the peak can be altered by varying the value of VR1. The peak frequency is about 100 Hz with VR1 at maximum value, rising to about 2 kHz or so when it is set for minimum resistance. The peak voltage gain does, unfortunately, vary slightly according to the setting of VR1, being about 12 dB at maximum resistance and over 20 dB at or near minimum resistance. Despite this the unit does give a good and perfectly acceptable waa-waa effect.

C1 is a supply decoupling capacitor and C6 provides D.C. blocking at the output of IC1. S1 is the straight forward on/off switch, and S2 can be used to cut out the waa-waa effect by breaking the circuit through VR1 and R5. R4, C4 and C5 then provide 100% negative feedback and the unit simply acts as a unity gain buffer amplifier. S2 can be a push to make — push to break foot operated switch so that it can be operated while playing the instrument. The current consumption of the circuit is only about 2 mA.

Construction

From the electrical viewpoint the unit is very simple and straight forward to construct. It is a little more difficult from the mechanical point of view since it is necessary to build a pedal mechanism so that VR1 can be operated by foot, leaving both hands free to play the guitar. Some designs use a rotary potentiometer, but the author found it to be much easier to employ a slider type in the unit. The simple mechanical arrangement outlined in Figure 6 can then be used. No precise constructional details of the pedal mechanism will be given as building this is really a matter of using ones initiative and ingenuity, and utilizing whatever suitable materials happen to be at hand or readily available to each individual constructor. It is important that the unit is strongly constructed though, since it will soon falter in use if it is at all flimsy. A strong case must be used and although a diecast

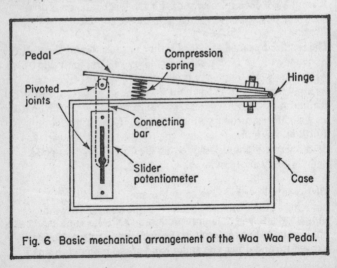

Fig. 6 Basic mechanical arrangement of the Waa Waa Pedal.

aluminium type would be ideal, it is unlikely that one having
sufficient depth will be obtainable. However, there are a
number of heavy duty metal cases available at present, and any
of these should be suitable provided they have adequate
dimensions.

Components Waa-Waa Pedal

Resistors
R1   4.7k
R2   4.7k
R3   47k
R4   220k
R5   820 ohms
VR1   100k 1in. carbon

Capacitors
C1   220 nF plastic foil
C2   100 μF 10V
C3   1 μF 10V
C4   10 nF plastic foil
C5   10 nF plastic foil
C6   10 μF 10V

Semiconductor
IC1   LF351 or equivalent

Switches
S1   S.P.S.T. type
S2   S.P.S.T. type

Miscellaneous
Case, PP3 size battery, battery connector, etc. Additional

Automatic Waa-Waa Unit

An automatic waa-waa unit produces much the same effect as a
manual unit, but the peak in the response is automatically
moved up and down the audio band at some predetermined

rate. With some types of automatic waa-waa units the effect is triggered as each new note is played, and with others, including the one described here, the effect is switched in and out as required using a footswitch. Automatic waa-waa units are perhaps a little less versatile and effective than there manual counterparts, but for the home constructor they have the advantage of being somewhat easier to construct due to the lack of any pedal mechanism. They are also a little easier to use.

The automatic version of the waa-waa unit is basically the same as the manual version, the difference being that VR1 and R5 are omitted from the original circuit, and are replaced by a voltage controlled resistance which is operated by a low frequency oscillator. This additional circuitry is shown in Figure 7.

The voltage controlled resistance is JFET Tr1's drain to source resistance. This is quite low when the gate of Tr1 is at or very close to the negative supply potential since the device will be biased into conduction. The actual resistance will be something in the region of 100 to 200 ohms, and together with the resistance of R5 this gives very much the same minimum resistance as is obtained in the manual version. If Tr1's gate is taken steadily positive, it will gradually become reversed biased and exhibit an increasing drain to source resistance. When fully cut off, the drain to source resistance is actually very high; something of the order of one thousand megohms. This is, of course, far higher than is required, and so R4 is used to shunt Tr1 in order to give the required maximum resistance of about 100k. Thus a control voltage applied to Tr1 gate will give the appropriate control resistance range and the waa-waa effect, provided the control signal has a suitable waveshape.

The control signal is generated by an ICM7555 device used in the astable mode. The ICM7555 is a CMOS version of the popular 555 timer I.C., and has the advantage in a battery operated circuit such as this of having only about one hundredth of the current consumption of the standard 555. A further advantage is that it is less likely to transmit noise spikes to other parts of the circuit since it does not draw a

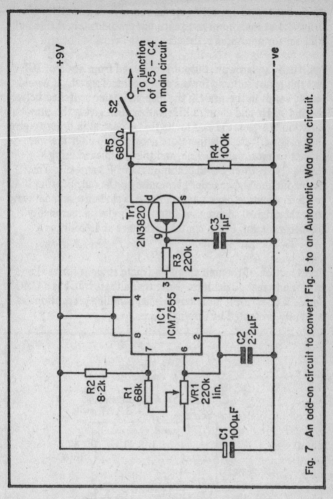

Fig. 7 An add-on circuit to convert Fig. 5 to an Automatic Waa Waa circuit.

high current spike from the supply as the output makes the transistion from the low to the high state, as does the standard 555. This last point is important in a sensitive audio circuit such as this one.

The operating frequency of IC1 is governed by the values of timing components R1, R2, VR1 and C2. By means of VR1 the frequency of operation can be varied from about 1.4 Hz with VR1 at maximum resistance to approximately 4.6 Hz with VR1 set for minimum resistance.

A virtually squarewave output is obtained from pin 3 of IC1, and this is not suitable for use as the control signal. It would simply result in the peak in the response being switched between about 100 Hz and about 2 kHz, rather than giving the smooth variation between the two limits that is needed in order to give the proper effect. It is therefore necessary to alter the wave-shape to a more suitable one, and this is achieved using a simple C − R filter which is comprised of R3 and C3. This filters out the higher order harmonics on the output from IC1, producing a waveshape much closer to a sine or triangular wave than the original squarewave input. This gives a reasonably smooth variation in the control resistance and produces a perfectly acceptable effect.

Construction of the unit should be quite straight forward and free of any real difficulties. Note that although IC1 is a CMOS device it does not require any special handling precautions as it is fully protected by internal circuitry.

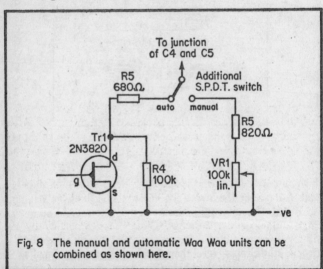

Fig. 8 The manual and automatic Waa Waa units can be combined as shown here.

If required, the waa-waa unit can be built as an automatic and manual unit by incorporating both the pedal/potentiometer set up and the control circuitry, with a switch being included so that the desired mode can be selected. This modification is outlined in Figure 8.

Additional Components for Automatic Operation

Resistors
R1   68k
R2   8.2k
R3   220k
R4   100k
R5   680 ohms
VR1   220k 1in. carbon

Capacitors
C1   100 μF 10V
C2   2.2 μF plastic foil
C3   1 μF plastic foil

Semiconductors
IC1   ICM7555
Tr1   2N3820

Sustain Unit

Normally a guitar produces an output signal that has a very high initial level which quickly decays to a medium level. After remaining at about this level for a comparitively long (although still rather short) time the signal steadily decays towards zero. The purpose of a sustain unit is to give a more stable output level, effectively increasing the maximum length of a note as well as changing the envelope characteristic of the signal.

As mentioned earlier, a fuzz box gives a form of sustain by simply boosting all input signals to the level where they are clipped, the clipping level then deciding the output signal's amplitude, the input level being irrelevant provided it is not too low to produce clipping. There are two main drawbacks of this very simple method. Firstly, and fairly obviously, the sustain effect is accompanied by the fuzz effect whether the latter is wanted or not. An improvement can be obtained by using a treble cut filter at the output of the unit so as to attenuate the higher frequency signals generated by the unit, but a considerable amount of distortion is still produced. A second drawback is that the initial "attack" of the guitar is lost, completely changing the sound of the instrument rather than just sustaining the output.

A slightly more complicated method of producing the sustain effect is to use a circuit of the compressor type and having fairly fast attack and decay times. This type of circuit is based on a voltage controlled amplifier, the control voltage for the V.C.A. being derived from the output signal via a rectifier and smoothing network. The circuit is arranged so that under quiescent and low signal conditions the gain of the unit is at maximum, and reduces at higher signal levels where a stronger control voltage is produced. Thus the higher the input signal level, the lower the gain of the circuit, resulting in a fairly stable output level.

This system only produces very low levels of distortion that are not of any significance, enabling chords to be played on the instrument without severe intermodulation distortion producing very dischordant results (as would occur if a clipping type sustain unit was to be used). Although the unit must be able to respond very quickly to changes in dynamic level in order to stabilise the output amplitude and give satisfactory results, it must inevitably have a significant response time that will prevent it from instantly responding to the initial high input level from the guitar. The unit can also be made to saturate at high signal levels so that some of the initial "attack" of the instrument is preserved.

The Circuit

Figure 9 shows the circuit diagram of the Sustain Unit. A low noise buffer stage is used at the input of the unit, and this

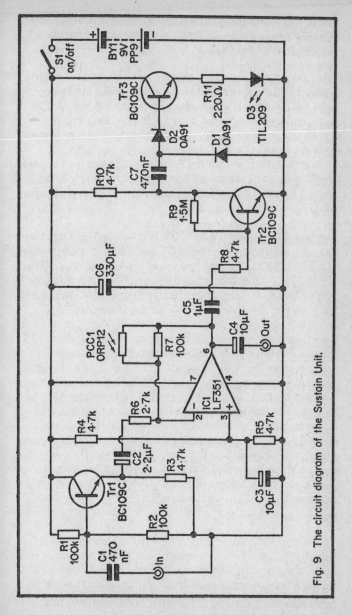

Fig. 9 The circuit diagram of the Sustain Unit.

23

uses Tr1 in the emitter follower mode. The purpose of this stage is merely to raise the input impedance of the circuit to a suitable level (about 47k).

The next stage of the unit is the voltage controlled amplifier. This is based on operational amplifier IC1 which is a low noise BIFET type. It is important for the circuit to have a low noise level since the output from a guitar can be less than 1 mV once the note has decayed somewhat, and an indifferent noise performance would give an extremely poor signal to noise ratio. IC1 is used in the inverting mode and has the non-inverting input biased to half the supply potential by R4 and R5. C3 provides decoupling at this input. C2 gives interstage coupling between Tr1 and IC1.

The closed loop voltage gain of IC1 is controlled by a negative feedback loop which consists of R6 and the combined resistance of R7 and PCC1. The gain is equal to the latter divided by the former, and is obviously largely dependant on the resistance of PCC1. This varies from about 10 megohms in total darkness to less than 100 ohms under very bright conditions. PCC1 is sealed off from the ambient lighting, and the light output from light emitting diode D3 is aimed at its light sensitive surface. D3 is fed from the emitter terminal of emitter follower transistor Tr3 via current limiting resistor R11. With no input voltage applied to Tr3 this device is cut off and D3 does not light up. PCC1 is then in total darkness and exhibits its maximum resistance. It therefore has very little shunting effect on R7 and the closed loop voltage gain of IC1 is 100 divided by 2.7, or approximately 37 in other words. If a strong positive bias is applied to Tr3 base, both Tr3 and D3 will become strongly forward biased. The light output from D3 then causes the resistance of PCC1 to fall to quite a low level, perhaps as little as 1k. In consequence the closed loop gain of IC1 drops to well below unity.

This arrangement thus gives the required voltage controlled amplifier action. This opto-isolator method may be unfamiliar to some readers, but it is quite often used these days as it has certain advantages over other methods. Probably the most important of these is that the photocell (which is of the cadmium sulphide type) is a true resistance, and does not introduce any significant distortion. A second major advantage is that the photocell is completely isolated from the controlling voltage, giving good freedom of design.

Returning now to the circuit operation, the control voltage is obtained by considerably amplifying the output from IC1 using Tr2 as a high gain common emitter amplifier, and then rectifying this signal using D1 and D2. It may seem as though there should be a smoothing capacitor from Tr3's base to the negative supply rail so that the pulsating D.C. output from D1 and D2 is integrated to a proper D.C. control voltage. However, this is not necessary due to the response times of the ORP12 photocell. This device responds very rapidly to increases in the light level from D3, but it responds far more slowly to reductions. This is a form of what is known as "hysteresis", and it means that PCC1 effectively responds to the average light output from D3, and not to individual light pulses. The response time of PCC1 is, of course, fast enough to properly stabilise the output and give the desired effect.

Figure 10 shows the compression effect of the prototype Sustain Unit. As can be seen from this, a 40 dB change in input level from 1 to 100 mV produces a change in output level of only about 9 dB. This level of compression is perfectly adequate for this application and gives good results in practice.

The component layout of the circuit is not too critical, but due to the high input sensitivity it is virtually essential to house the unit in a metal case which should be earthed to the negative supply rail. This will then provide overall screening of the unit and prevent stray pick-up of mains hum and other electrical interference. The noise level of the prototype unit seemed to be suitably low, but an improvement can be made by adding a capacitor of about 330 pf across R7. This attenuates the high frequency response of the circuit somewhat when the gain of the unit is at or near maximum (which is also when the background noise level is at maximum). The treble attenuation reduces the level of high frequency noise on the output, this noise being the most noticeable and objection-

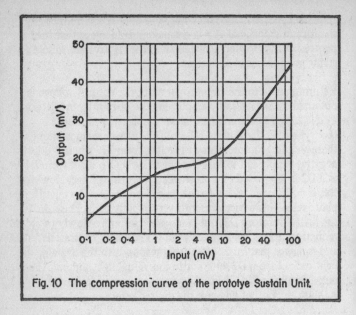

Fig. 10 The compression curve of the prototye Sustain Unit.

able. No significant treble cut or noise reduction will be given at lower gain levels since PCC1 then produces a much lower feedback resistance, making the shunting effect of the additional capacitor of no consequence at audio frequencies. However, the noise level of the circuit is much lower when it is providing low levels of gain, making any noise reduction unnecessary. Thus the effect on the frequency response of the unit is no more than is absolutely necessary.

In use results will almost certainly be best with the volume control on the guitar (if fitted) set at maximum. The only exceptions might be guitars which have an unusually high output level, and then results may possibly be better with the volume control backed off somewhat. A little experimentation will soon show if this is the case or not. The overall system will have a very high level of gain and care must be taken to ensure that there is enough separation between the pick-up and the loudspeakers if a non-humbucking pick-up is used. It may also be necessary to slightly back off the volume control in some cases, although this should obviously be avoided if

26

possible. A certain amount of stray feedback can tend to aid the sustain effect, but this is not recommended as it can lead to a very poor frequency response, and if this system should slip into oscillation it is possible that damage could be caused to the amplifier or speakers.

Components Sustain Unit

Resistors
R1   100k
R2   100k
R3   4.7k
R4   4.7k
R5   4.7k
R6   2.7k
R7   100k
R8   4.7k
R9   1.5M
R10   4.7k
R11   220 ohms

Capacitors
C1   470 nF plastic foil
C2   2.2 μF 10V
C3   10 μF 10V
C4   10 μF 10V
C5   1 μF plastic foil
C6   330 μF 10V
C7   470 nF plastic foil

Photocell
PCC1 ORP12

Semiconductors
IC1   LF351 or equivalent
Tr1   BC109C
Tr2   BC109C
Tr3   BC109C
D1   OA91
D2   OA91

D3   TIL209

Switch
S1   S.P.S.T. type

Miscellaneous
Case, PP9 size battery, battery connector, etc.

Opto-Isolator

Obviously PCC1 and D3 must be mounted so that as much of
the light output from the diode as possible is directed onto the
sensitive surface of the photocell. This will be achieved with
the two components aligned and with their front surfaces
virtually touching one another. For optimum results a signal
generator can be used to feed a tone into the unit (about 10 to
500 mV R.M.S. in amplitude), an audio millivolt meter can
be used to monitor the output level, and D3 and PCC1 are then
orientated to produce the minimum possible output level.
Good results should be obtained without going through this
procedure though.

Of course, PCC1 must be shielded from the ambient lighting,
but it should not be necessary to make any special arrangements
in this respect as presumably the case of the unit will provide
this shielding.

CHAPTER 2

GENERAL EFFECTS UNITS

The first chapter dealt with effects units that are primarily
(although not exclusively) used with guitars. This second
chapter will cover a number of effects units that are of more
general application, and are in general use with a variety of
instruments.

Tremolo Generator

Probably the most widely used of these general effects units
are tremolo generators. Tremolo merely consists of amplitude
modulating the input signal with a very low frequency. In
other words, the strength of the input signal is varied up and
down at a rate of just a few Hertz. This could of course be
done manually using a simple volume control type circuit, but
this is not usually convenient in practice, and some automatic
means is normally employed.

The circuit diagram of the tremolo unit appears in Figure 11.
The input signal is applied by way of D.C. blocking capacitor
C2 to an electronic attenuator which is comprised of R1, R2
and Tr1. When the gate of Tr1 is at or close to the negative
supply rail potential, the device is biased hard into conduction
and it exhibits a drain to source resistance of only about one
hundred ohms or so. This causes quite high losses through the
attenuator with the input signal being reduced to roughly one
twentieth of its previous level (i.e. a loss of about 26 dB).

If the gate of Tr1 is taken several volts positive with respect to
the negative rail, the device will be switched off and then
exhibits a drain to source resistance of about one thousand
megohms. The losses through the attenuator are then
extremely small and not really of any significance. Loading
by the next stage of the unit does actually introduce a more
substantial loss through the attenuator of a few dB., but this

29

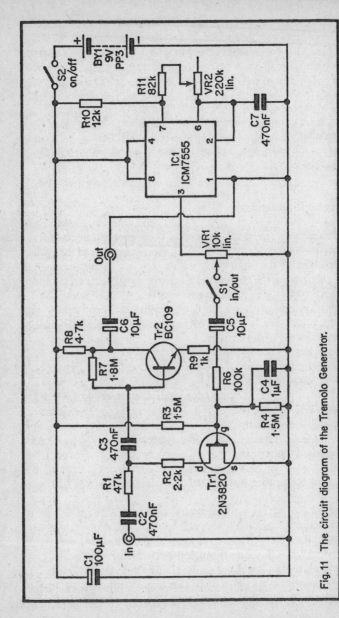

Fig.11 The circuit diagram of the Tremolo Generator.

30

still permits a variation in gain of over 20 dB to be obtained by the control voltage applied to Tr1 gate. The value of R1 is chosen to give an input impedance that is high enough to give a good match to any normal guitar, organ, or other instrument. The input impedance actually varies somewhat with changes in the bias applied to Tr1, but the minimum input impedance is approximately 50k.

The output from the attenuator is coupled to the output socket via an amplifier stage which has two functions. Firstly it acts as a buffer stage so that excessive loading of the attenuator, producing only a very limited tremolo effect, cannot occur if the unit is used to feed into a low input impedance. Secondly, it must provide a certain amount of gain so that the circuit does not simply vary the gain downwards from unity and then back up to unity again, but provides a variation centered on approximately unity gain. Otherwise the losses through the circuit could make it impossible to obtain sufficient volume from the equipment.

The necessary gain is provided by Tr2 which is a high gain, low noise device used in the common emitter mode. R7 is the base bias resistor, R8 is the collector load, and C3 provides D.C. blocking at the input of this stage. The full voltage gain available from Tr2 is not required in this application; a voltage gain of only about four or five times being sufficient. An unbypassed emitter resistor is therefore included so as to introduce a large amount of negative feedback to this stage and thus reduce the voltage gain to the required level. The voltage gain of the amplifier is actually about 4.7 times. The negative feedback has the advantage of reducing noise and distortion generated by the amplifier to insignificant proportions. It also boosts the input impedance of the amplifier to about 100k so that there are no problems with excessive loading of the attenuator. The amplified signal at Tr2 collector is passed to the output socket by way of D.C. blocking capacitor C6.

Ideally a sinewave signal would be used as the control voltage for Tr1, but a good quality variable frequency sinewave oscillator would considerably complicate the circuit. Instead, a rectangular waveshape is generated by a simple astable circuit, and the output is then filtered to remove the higher frequency harmonics and give a more suitable waveshape. If used without filtering the rectangular waveform would merely switch the attenuator between its maximum and minimum gain settings, giving a totally unsatisfactory effect. The filtering produces a roughly triangular waveform which gives a more smooth variation in gain, and a perfectly acceptable tremolo effect.

The rectangular signal is generated by the astable circuit based on IC1, an ICM7555 device being used in this position. This is used in the standard 555 style astable circuit, with R10, R11, VR2 and C7 acting as the timing components. By adjusting VR2 the frequency of the tremolo can be adjusted from about 17 Hz with VR2 at minimum resistance down to about 5 Hz with VR2 at maximum resistance. The output from pin 3 of IC1 feeds direct into VR1 which controls the amplitude of the control signal, and thus also acts as the tremolo depth control.

From the slider of VR1 the signal is coupled to the filter through S1. This can be used to disconnect the control signal and mute the tremolo effect when required. R6 and C4 are the low pass filter, and a simple single section R — C circuit is all that is required here. C5 provides D.C. blocking and ensures that a proper alternating voltage is applied to Tr1's gate. R3 and R4 form a potential divider which biases the gate terminal of Tr1 to about half the supply potential. Without this bias the input signal would not cover the appropriate section of Tr1's transfer characteristic, and the tremolo effect would either be only produced over a small part of the control signal's waveform (giving a poor and shallow effect) or it would not be produced at all.

S2 is the on/off switch and C1 is a supply decoupling capacitor. The current consumption of the unit is less than 2 mA.

From the constructional viewpoint there should be no real problems with this project, but try to keep the oscillator circuitry reasonably well separated from the rest of the unit so that stray coupling does not cause harmonics of the fundamental frequency to break through to the output. This is especially important where the unit is used with low level signals, such as those produced by a guitar pick-up. If used with a high level signal, such as that normally obtained from an organ, then the layout will not really be very critical in this respect.

The circuit can handle signal levels of up to a couple of volts or so peak to peak without causing serious distortion.

Components Tremolo Generator

Resistors
R1   47k
R2   2.2k
R3   1.5M
R4   1.5M
R6   100k
R7   1.8M
R8   4.7k
R9   1k
R10   12k
R11   82k
VR1   10k 1in. carbon
VR2   220k 1in. carbon

Capacitors
C1   100 μF 10V
C2   470 nF plastic foil
C3   470 nF plastic foil
C4   1 μF plastic foil
C5   10 μF 25V
C6   10 μF 10V
C7   470 nF plastic foil

Semiconductors
IC1   ICM7555
Tr1   2N3820
Tr2   BC109

Switches
S1   S.P.S.T.
S2   S.P.S.T.

Miscellaneous
Case, component panel, battery, battery connector, etc.

Reverberation Unit

In simple terms, reverberation is the effect produced by sound waves bouncing around the interior of a room. This does not give one distinct echo, but a whole multitude of echoes that combine together to produce a jumble of sounds. In most rooms the reverberation time is very short because the furnishings tend to absorb sounds, rapidly damping down the echoes. In large halls though, a reverberation time of two or three seconds is often obtained, and this gives a very rich sound to many types of music.

Reverberation can be artificially added to a signal where it is not practical to obtain natural reverberation of the desired decay time. There are a number of ways in which this effect can be achieved, but the most popular method and probably the most simple is to use a spring-line unit plus the appropriate additional circuitry. Basically a spring line consists of two transducers joined by a spring. One tranducer is fed with the input signal which it converts into a sound wave signal that is sent down the spring. The other transducer receives these soundwaves and converts them back into an electrical signal. However, the waves travel relatively slowly down the spring giving a delaying effect. Furthermore, the waves are repeatedly reflected backwards and forwards along the spring giving the required multiple echoing effect. This gives an output from the second transducer that is a very good approximation of the sound produced by the reverberation of a large hall. Of course, in most cases it is not just the reverberation signal that is required, but the ordinary signal plus a certain amount of added reverberation. The circuit must therefore include a mixer section so that the main and reverberation signals can be mixed at the desired comparative levels.

The circuit diagram is shown in Figure 12. Considerable losses are produced through a spring-line unit making it necessary to use a drive signal of a few hundred milliwatts and then considerably amplify the output from the unit in order to obtain a reasonably high signal level. In this circuit the spring-line is driven by an audio power amplifier based on the TBA820M integrated circuit. The input signal is applied to this via D.C. blocking capacitor and level control VR1. Note that no D.C. blocking capacitor is needed between VR1 and the input of IC1. In fact it is essential not to add a capacitor here because VR1 provides the input bias for IC1. There is an internal feedback resistor between the output of IC1 and the inverting input at pin 2 (the input signal is applied to the non-inverting input). An external resistor and D.C. blocking capacitor are used to decouple some of the feedback and set the voltage gain of the circuit at the required level. This discrete network is formed by R1 and C2, the specified value for R1 setting the voltage gain at approximately 22 times. R2 and C4 are bootstrapping components which help to give a high peak to peak output voltage swing (and thus also output power) from the circuit. C3, R3 and C6 aid the stability of the circuit. C5 couples the output from the amplifier to the input transducer of the spring-line.

The spring-line is a ready made component having magnetic input and output transducers. Its output transducer feeds one input of a conventional operational amplifier mixer circuit which utilises BIFET operational amplifier IC2. When S2 is in the closed position, the input signal is fed to the other input of the mixer circuit. This gives the required mixing of the main and reverberation signals, the amount of the latter that is added to the ordinary signal being controlled by means of VR1. The output from the spring-line unit will normally be at a much lower level than the main signal. R6 is therefore given a much lower value than R7 so that the output from the spring line is boosted in comparison to the main signal. In fact, R7 and R8 set the voltage gain for the main signal at unity, whereas R6 and R8 give a voltage gain of ten times (20 dB) for the output from the spring-line. This enables high levels of reverberation

35

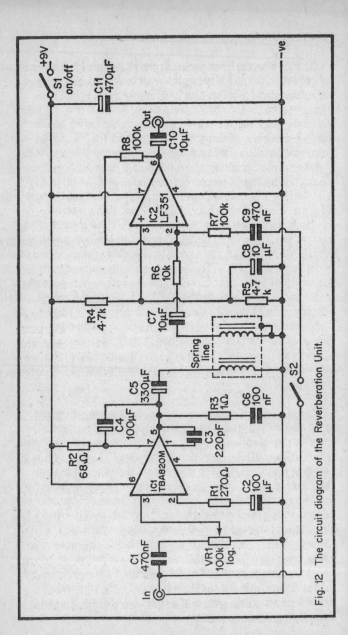

Fig. 12 The circuit diagram of the Reverberation Unit.

36

signal to be obtained when required.

With S2 set in the open position, the main signal is disconnected from the mixer circuitry, and then only the reverberation signal is obtained at the output. IC2 then acts as a simple x10 amplifier stage rather than as a mixer.

D.C. blocking at the output is provided by C10, and supply decoupling is given by C11. S1 is an ordinary on/off switch. The quiescent current consumption of the circuit is only about 6 or 7 mA, but this increases substantially if a high level of reverberation is required, as the class B output stage of IC1 may then have to provide a few hundred milliwatts of output power. This can lead to an average current drain of 50 mA or more. It is therefore advisable to power the project from a fairly large 9 volt battery, such as a PP7 or PP9 type.

Few problems should be encountered when constructing the reverberation unit. A fairly large case is needed due to the length of the spring-line unit, which is actually something over 200 mm. long. A number of good quality metal instrument cases of a suitable size are available at quite reasonable prices. The input and output connections of the spring-line unit are clearly marked, and it is essential to connect the unit the right way round. The input and output transducers have totally different impedances (16 ohms and 10k respectively), and so the unit is definately not reversible. It should be noted that one of the output terminals of the spring-line is ready connected to the metal casing of the unit by a soldertag. This is the output terminal that connects to the negative rail, and not the one that connects to C7. The connections to the input transducer can be made either way round incidentally.

In use, the unit should really be connected in a part of the overall setup where it handles a fairly high level signal, say in the region of 50 to 750 mV R.M.S. It will work using a low level input, say from a microphone or a guitar, but the signal to noise ratio is not likely to be particularly good. In most cases of this type it would be of considerable benefit to interpose a suitable preamplifier between the signal source and the reverberation unit.

It should be borne in mind that except with low level inputs of about 100 mV R.M.S. or less, turning VR1 well up towards maximum will cause IC1 to overload and clip the signal at its output. Therefore, take care not to advance this control too far, as doing so will not give a higher level of reverberation, but will simply cause the output signal to be rather distorted.

Components Reverberation Unit

Resistors
R1   270 ohms
R2   68 ohms
R3   1 ohm
R4   4.7k
R5   4.7k
R6   10k
R7   100k
R8   100k
VR1 100k log. carbon

Capacitors
C1   470 nF plastic foil
C2   100 μF 10V
C3   220 pF ceramic plate
C4   100 μF 10V
C5   330 μF 10V
C6   100 nF plastic foil
C7   10 μF 25V
C8   10 μF 10V
C9   470 nF plastic foil
C10 10 μF 10V
C11 470 μF 10V

Semiconductors
IC1 TBA820M
IC2 LF351

Switches
S1   S.P.S.T.
S2   S.P.S.T.

Miscellaneous
Case, component panel, short spring-line unit, battery, etc.

Automatic Phaser

Although the phasing effect is of comparitively recent origin,
it has quickly become very popular, and will probably be
familiar to most readers. In a way it can be considered as being
the inverse of the waa-waa effect, as the waa-waa effect consists
of boosting a narrow band of frequencies, and varying the
centre frequency of the boosted band over the audio range.
The phasing effect is produced by having a narrow band of
high attenuation, or rejection notch filtering, as this is normally
termed. This attenuation notch is either manually or automatically swept up and down the audio frequency spectrum to
produce the phasing effect. Simple phasers have just one
rejection notch, but some of the more sophisticated units have
two, three, or even more notches. In general, the greater the
number of notches the better the effect that is produced
(within reason). However, multiple notch types tend to be
rather expensive and complicated. Also, multinotch types
normally use multistage circuits, the number of stages being
proportional to the number of notches obtained (two stages
per notch in the standard type of circuit). There is naturally
some loss of quality through each of these (active) stages, and
so the more notches that are obtained, the greater the loss of
quality that is likely to occur.

A few experiments showed that quite a good effect could be
produced using a single notch phaser, and that such a unit
could be built quite inexpensively employing a very simple
circuit. Furthermore, such a unit gives no significant loss of
quality.

The Circuit

The phaser circuit is shown in Figure 13. The filter uses a well
known configuration which has a Wien network and a phase
splitter, although the circuit is rather unusual in that two

39

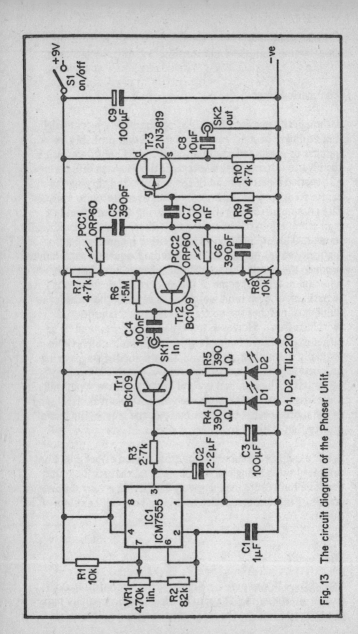

Fig. 13 The circuit diagram of the Phaser Unit.

photocells are used to vary the frequency of the rejection notch, rather than the more usual twin gang potentiometer. The use of photocells as the variable resistances enables the operating frequency of the filter to be automatically swept up and down using an opto-isolator technique.

If we look at the circuit in more detail now, Tr2 is used as the phase splitter stage. R8 introduces a considerable amount of negative feedback to Tr2 if it is considered in the common emitter mode, and R8 is actually adjusted to give the unit a voltage gain of fractionally less than unity from its base to collector terminals. If Tr2 is considered as an emitter follower stage, there will also be slightly less than unity voltage gain from its base to emitter terminals. However, whereas a 180 degree phase change is produced through a common emitter amplifier, there is zero phase shift through an emitter follower type. Thus an input applied to Tr2's base will be out-of-phase at its collector, and in-phase at its emitter. The two output signals will be at precisely the same amplitude provided R8 is adjusted correctly.

One section of the Wien network is formed by PCC1 and C5, the other section being comprised of PCC1 and C6. At a certain frequency there will be zero phase shift through the upper section of the Wien network. Provided the valves in the lower section of the Wien circuit are the same as those in the upper section, which they are, there will also be zero phase shift through the lower section at this frequency. The two outputs from the Wien network are connected together so that the two signals are mixed. The two signals will precisely cancel one another out at the zero phase shift frequency of the Wien network, since they are at the same amplitude and are of opposite phase. This give the required rejection notch in the frequency response of the unit.

At frequencies away from the operating one of the Wien network there is a different amount of phase shift through the two sections. This gives only partial cancelling of the output signals, and only a marginal loss of gain through the circuit. In actual fact the gain of the circuit is virtually unity just above and below the frequency of the rejection notch.

41

For the filter to operate well it must feed into a high impedance load, and a buffer stage using Tr3 in the source follower mode has therefore been used to ensure that the filter operates into a suitable load. It actually provides an input impedance of about 10 megohms. C7 gives interstage coupling and D.C. blocking. C8 is the output D.C. blocking capacitor.

The sweep oscillator uses IC1 in the standard 555 type astable configuration. R1 is made low in comparison to the timing resistance between pins 6 and 7 of the IC1 so that the output signal is virtually a square wave having a 1 to 1 mark space ratio. VR1 enables the operating frequency of the oscillator to be varied from about 1.4 Hz to about 8 Hz.

Of course, a square wave signal is not suitable for use as the control signal because it would merely switch the filter between two operating frequencies, rather than sweeping the operating frequency up and down over the audio spectrum. C2, R3 and C3 are therefore used to provide low pass filtering which processes the output from IC1 to produce a more acceptable wave shape (roughly triangular).

This signal is then fed into the base of emitter follower transistor, Tr1. This drives light emitting diodes D1 and D2 from its emitter, via separate current limiting resistors R4 and R5. The light output from D1 is directed at the sensitive surface of PCC1, while the output from D2 is directed at the sensitive surface of PCC2. Thus, as the oscillator causes the light output from D1 and D2 to rise and fall, the resistances of PCC1 and PCC2 decrease and increase. As their resistances vary, so does the operating frequency of the Wien network, and the rejection notch is swept up and down the audio range in the required manner, producing the phasing effect.

On/off switching is provided by S1, and C9 is the only supply decoupling component that is needed. The current consumption of the unit obviously varies with changes in the brightness of the two L.E.D.s, but on average it is about 25 mA. It is recommended that a large or medium sized 9 volt battery (PP6, PP9 etc.) should therefore be used to power the unit.

Bypass switching is not shown in Figure 13, but if desired this can be added. All that is required is a S.P.D.T. switch arranged so that the output socket is connected either to the input socket, or to the negative side of C8, depending upon the switch position.

Construction of the unit should be fairly simple, the only point requiring any amplification being the arranging of the opto-isolators. The ORP60 is an "end − on" type cell, and it has the same body diameter as the TIL220 (0.2 in. red) L.E.D.s specified for D1 and D2. Each photocell can therefore be fairly easily mounted end on to its corresponding L.E.D., with a length of P.V.C. sleeving of the appropriate inside diameter or a band of insulation tape being used to fix the two devices together. This sleeve can also be used to provide a light-proof housing for the opto-isolators, so that the unit will work properly even when removed from its casing, or if it is housed in a non-light-proof case.

Only one adjustment needs to be made to the finished unit, and that is to set R8 to give the deepest notch obtainable. Initially R8 is set at about half maximum, which is approximately the correct setting. With an input signal of some kind, R8 can then be set to give the best phasing effect. A signal containing a wide range of frequencies is ideal for use as the test signal when making this adjustment, suitable signals being a low frequency square wave or white noise. An F.M. radio or tuner can be used as a white noise source if it is tuned off-station. A sinewave signal can be used, but R8 is then adjusted for the most pronounced dip in signal level as the filter sweeps through the frequency of the input signal. If this method is used, it will probably be easier if VR1 is adjusted for the lowest sweep frequency.

A music or voice signal can be used as the test signal if one of the methods mentioned above cannot be used. Be careful to adjust R8 for the correct effect though, as adjusting it too low in value will produce a strong effect which might be accepted as the phasing effect. In fact it is not, and is actually more like a waa-waa effect. The phasing effect is rather more subtle and less pronounced.

43

Resistors
R1   10k
R2   82k
R3   2.7k
R4   390 ohms
R5   390 ohms
R6   1.5M
R7   4.7k
R8   10k 0.1 watt preset
R9   10M
R10 4.7k
VR1 470 1in. carbon

Photocells
PCC1 ORP60
PCC2 ORP60

Capacitors
C1   1 μF plastic foil
C2   2.2 μF 25V
C3   100 μF 10V
C4   100 nF plastic foil
C5   390 pF polystyrene
C6   390 pF polystyrene
C7   100 nF plastic foil
C8   10 μF 10V
C9   100 μF 10V

Semiconductors
IC1 ICM7555
Tr1 BC109
Tr2 BC109
Tr3 2N3819
D1   TIL220
D2   TIL220

Switch
S1   S.P.S.T.

Miscellaneous
Case, component board, battery, battery connector, wire etc.

Audio Modulator

We have already encountered an example of a simple modulator circuit in an earlier project; the Tremolo Generator of Figure 11. Here the input of the modulator was fed from an internal low frequency oscillator so that the amplitude of the processed signal varied up and down in sympathy with the control voltage from the oscillator. This simple modulator has no internal oscillator, and a number of interesting effects can be produced by feeding the appropriate type of signal to the modulation input.

It should perhaps be explained that there are various types of audio modulator. The simplest ones, including the one described here, are of the non-balanced type, and with these, frequencies applied at either input appear at the output. Single balanced modulators have only frequencies at one or other of the inputs appearing at the output, plus the frequencies generated by the modulation process of course. Double balanced modulators have only the signals generated by the modulation process appearing at the output.

In order to produce some effects well it is necessary to have a single balanced, and occasionally a double balanced modulator, but most of the simpler effects can be obtained using a simple non-balanced type such as the one described here. It can, for example, be used to modulate one tone onto another so as to produce more complex sounds. It can also be used to modulate a voice signal onto music. Obviously, by using a low frequency modulation signal a tremolo effect can be obtained.

The unit is based on the MC3340P electronic attenuator I.C., as can be seen by referring to the circuit diagram of Figure 14. The gain through this device can be controlled by a resistance connected between its control terminal (pin 2) and the negative supply rail, and (or) a control voltage applied to this terminal. In this case the gain of the device is set at roughly -7 dB by

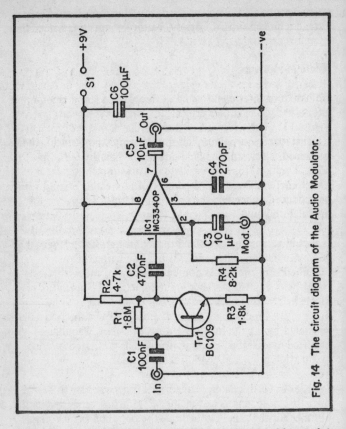

Fig. 14 The circuit diagram of the Audio Modulator.

control resistance R4. The gain of IC1 can be varied by applying a control voltage to pin 2 by way of D.C. blocking capacitor C3. A control voltage of about 2 volts peak to peak is needed in order to give the maximum available gain variation of ± 20 dB. This control range is more than adequate for most applications.

Tr1 is used in a simple low gain common emitter stage which compensates for the 7 dB loss through IC1, and gives the circuit a nominal voltage gain of unity. C4 rolls of the frequency response of the MC3340P at R.F., and aids the stability of the circuit. C1, C2 and C5 are all D.C. blocking

46

capacitors, while C6 is a supply decoupling capacitor. S1 provides on/off switching, and the current consumption of the circuit is approximately 8 mA.

The input impedance of the circuit is about 300k, and the output impedance is quite low as the MC3340P has an emitter follower output stage. The input impedance at the modulation input is roughly 6k.

The unit is very simple and straight forward, and is unlikely to present any constructional difficulties.

Output levels of up to 6 volts peak to peak can be handled by the circuit before clipping and serious distortion occurs. However, when the modulation input is fully driven, the unit will at times be providing a voltage gain of about 20 dB (10 times), and the input should then not exceed 600 mV peak to peak if clipping is to be avoided.

Components Audio Modulator

Resistors
R1   1.8M
R2   4.7k
R3   1.8k
R4   8.2k

Capacitors
C1   100 nF plastic foil
C2   470 nF plastic foil
C3   10 μF 10V
C4   270 pF ceramic plate
C5   10 μF 10V
C6   100 μF 10V

Semiconductors
IC1   MC3340P
Tr1   BC109

Switch
S1   S.P.S.T.

Miscellaneous
Case, component board, battery, battery connector, wire, etc.

Envelope Shaper

An envelope shaper is used to vary the dynamic level of a
signal to give some desired effect. For example, the output of
a pulse generator can be processed by an envelope shaper to
give a sound that is similar to that produced by a harpsichord.
Simply switching the pulse generator on and off would not
produce the desired effect because the signal would have
virtually instant attack and decay. In other words, as soon as
the key was depressed the output level would almost instantly
jump to full amplitude. Similarly, the moment the key was
released the signal would almost instantly cease. This is not
what happens with a harpsichord, a piano, or similar instruments. With these the output amplitude quickly rises to a
maximum intensity, somewhat more slowly (although still
fairly quickly) decays to a lower level, sustains at this level for
a short while and then dies away to nothing. By using an
input waveform of the appropriate type, and an envelope
shaper that varies the dynamic level of the signal in the
appropriate way, it is thus possible to electronically simulate
conventional instruments.

Furthermore, using tone generators and envelope shapers it is
possible to produce new sounds and effects, and this field is
not simply confined to the simulation of conventional musical
instruments.

Envelope shapers that give an accurate simulation of pianos,
harpsichords, etc., tend to be rather complex, often using a
dozen or more active components and a large amount of passive
circuitry as well. However, quite good percussion effects can
be obtained using simple envelope shaper circuits, and other
interesting effects can be produced using such circuits.

The circuit diagram of a simple envelope chaper circuit is shown in Figure 15. The circuit is triggered at the beginning of each note by S1, which in practice will normally be a set of keyboard switches wired in parallel. If the unit is used to provide special effects in conjunction with a tone generator or white noise generator, then S1 would be an ordinary push to make, non-locking type switch.

Like the previous circuit, this one is based on the MC3340P electronic attenuator (IC1). The gain of this device under quiescent conditions is controlled by variable resistor R1, and can be varied from a typical level of 13 dB with R1 at or near minimum resistance, to about -80 dB with it at maximum resistance.

IC2 is an ICM7555 device used in the standard 555 monostable mode. A monostable multivibrator produces an output pulse of a duration that is set by a C — R timing network, when it has been triggered by a suitable input pulse. In this circuit R4 and C7 are the timing circuit, and they produce an output pulse of about 1.1 mS in duration since the output pulse length is approximately 1.1 CR. The circuit must be triggered by very briefly taking the trigger input (pin 2) below two thirds of the supply potential. This will happen if S1 is depressed, as C6 will initially be discharged, and the trigger input will be taken to the negative supply rail potential. C6 quickly charges via R5 though, so that no matter how long S1 is depressed, the trigger input is only taken below two thirds of the supply potential for a fraction of a millisecond. This is important, because if the trigger input was to be below the trigger threshold voltage at the end of the output pulse, the pulse would be elongated, and would not cease until the trigger input went back above the trigger threshold voltage. Therefore, simply connecting S1 from the trigger input to the negative supply rail would not give satisfactory operation. R5 ensures that the trigger input is taken above the trigger threshold voltage under quiescent conditions. R3 quickly discharges C6 when S1 is released, so that the circuit triggers once again when S1 is next operated. This discharge time is made

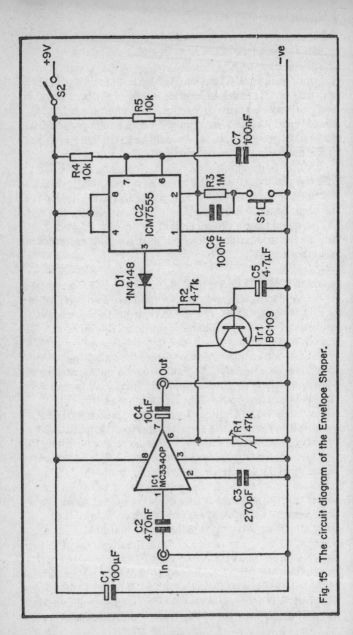

Fig. 15 The circuit diagram of the Envelope Shaper.

sufficiently long to prevent contact bounce from causing spurious operation of the circuit though.

The positive output pulse from IC2 is fed to the base of common emitter switching transistor Tr1 by way of D1 and R2. The pulse causes Tr1 to be switched hard on almost at once, although a small delay is provided by C5 in conjunction with the forward resistance of D1 and the resistance of R2. As Tr1 begins to conduct, it reduces the voltage at the control terminal of IC1, quickly pushing the gain of this device to its maximum level.

The circuit does not stay in this state for long due to the short duration of the output pulse from IC2. When this pulse ceases there is no longer a bias current for Tr1 through D1 and R2, and so Tr1 obviously switches off. It is delayed somewhat though, since C5 holds Tr1 in the on state until it has discharged to a voltage that is insufficient to do so. C5 discharges more slowly than it originally took to charge, because Tr1 is operating at only a very low collector current, and therefore has a fairly high input impedance. C5 cannot discharge through R2, D1 and the output circuitry of IC2 because D1 blocks any current flow in this direction. Its only discharge path is into the base circuit of Tr1. Of course, as Tr1 begins to switch off once again, the control voltage fed to IC1 is returned to its original level, as is the gain of the circuit.

Thus the required percussion effect is produced with the high initial gain of the circuit giving the initial transient. The signal then more slowly decays to a level set by R1 as the charge on C5 collapses.

On/off switching is provided by S2, and C1 is the only supply decoupling component that is needed. The circuit has a current consumption of approximately 6 to 7 mA.

Once again, there should be no constructional problems with this project as it is very straight forward in all respects. It is really a type of circuit that is ideal for those who like to experiment, as different sounds and effects can be produced by altering certain component values. For example, the length for which the initial high output level is sustained can be altered by changing the value giving a longer initial burst of signal. The speed at which the signal decays can be varied by altering the value of C5, the decay time being roughly proportional to the value of this component. A weird effect can be produced by giving the signal a slow initial build up, and this can be achieved by considerably raising the value of R2. By replacing D1 with a wire link a further change in the envelope shape will be obtained, as the signal will then have a decay time that is shorter than the attack time.

The effect produced by the unit can also be varied by adjusting R1. With this at maximum resistance the output will decay to what for all practical purposes can be considered as zero. Most people will probably prefer the effect obtained with this set for a minimum decay level of about 20 dB or so though. Quite a pleasant effect is produced with R1 set for a decay level only a few dB below the peak output level.

Apart from use with an organ, interesting effects can be obtained using an envelope generator in conjunction with tone and noise generators. These effects can be further enhanced by using, say, a phaser between the signal source and the envelope shaper. This is really a matter of experimenting with various combinations so as to find those that produce the best and most interesting effects.

Components Envelope Shaper

Resistors
R1   47k 0.1 watt preset
R2   4.7k
R3   1M
R4   10k
R5   10k

Capacitors
C1   100 μF 10V
C2   470 nF plastic foil
C3   270 pF ceramic plate

C4   10 μF 25V
C5   4.7 μF 25V
C6   100 nF plastic foil
C7   100 nF plastic foil

Semiconductors
IC1   MC3340P
IC2   ICM7555
Tr1   BC109
D1   1N4148

Switches
S1   Push to make, release to break type (see text).
S2   S.P.S.T.

Miscellaneous
Case, circuit board, battery, battery connector, wire, etc.

CHAPTER 3

SOUND GENERATOR PROJECTS

The two previous chapters have concentrated on circuits which
give special effects when used to process the output from a
musical instrument or other signal source. It really goes beyond
the scope of a book of simple circuits to give details of
sophisticated organs, synthesisers, etc., with detailed notes on
usage. However, details of some interesting and very useful
sound generator projects will be given in this chapter, and a
great deal of pleasure can be had by experimenting with these
and using them in conjunction with effects units. A great deal
about the production of electronic music can be learned in
this way, and this experience will be invaluable if progress is
made to more complex equipment at some later date.

White Noise Generator

Although in most electronic systems noise is considered to be
a nuisance, and something to be cut to a minimum, there are
some applications where noise can be put to good use. It is
used for testing hi-fi systems, loudspeakers, R.F. amplifiers,
and, of greater relevance here, it is used in the production of
special effects and the simulation of certain sounds. It can, for
instance, be used to produce wind like effects in electronic
music, or simulate the sound of a gunshot, if suitably processed.

The type of noise normally generated by electronic components is called white noise, and this has the same amount of
energy in frequency bands of the same width. In other words,
there is the same amount of signal level between say 1 kHz and
2 kHz as there is between 19 kHz and 20 kHz. This gives white
noise an effective high frequency bias, and produces the well
known hissing sound of the background noise that occurs in
audio circuits.

White noise can be filtered to produce so called coloured noise,
and one of the most common forms of coloured noise, in fact

probably the most common, is pink noise. This is filtered to progressively attenuate the noise at higher frequencies, giving a sound that seems to have a more uniform level over the audio range. This type of noise has equal energy over bands of equal percentage width. In other words, there would be the same energy in the signals from 100 Hz to 300 Hz, as there would in those from 1 kHz to 3 kHz, as each band has a width of 200%.

The Circuit

The circuit diagram of a white noise generator for use at audio frequencies is shown in Figure 16. Virtually any electronic component will generate white noise, and in a circuit of this type it is merely a matter of choosing one that provides a good output over the required frequency range. Experiments with various diodes and transistors showed that germanium transistors seemed to give the highest output. Audio types such as OC72s, OC81Ds and OC81s seemed to give good results, but R.F. types such as AF117 gave a much stronger output, and and AF114 V.H.F. device gave an even more substantial output. The reason for the higher output from R.F. and V.H.F. types is simply because these are not optimised for a good audio noise performance, but for low noise at their intended operating frequencies.

Tr1 is the noise transistor, and it is connected as a straight forward common emitter amplifier having R1 as the base bias resistor and R2 as the collector load. Of course, no input is applied to the base, and the output signal from the collector is only the noise generated by the device.

This noise is at a fairly low level, and in order to produce an output signal of useful proportions it is necessary to considerably amplify it. Tr2 is used as a high gain common emitter amplifier which gives over 40 dB of voltage gain. On the prototype this gave an output of about 250 mV R.M.S. using an AF114 noise transistor. About 150 to 200 mV was obtained when AF117 types were tried, and audio output types (OC81, OC72, AC176 etc.) gave about 50 to 100 mV

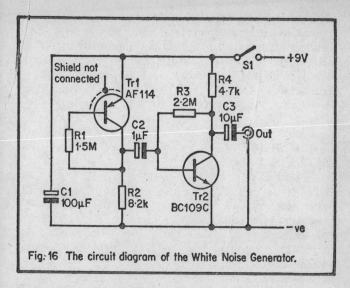

Fig. 16 The circuit diagram of the White Noise Generator.

R.M.S. Virtually any germanium p.n.p. device should give good results, but the specified type should be employed if a high output level is needed.

The only control for the unit is on/off switch S1. The current consumption of the circuit is only about 1.5 mA.

Only one special point needs to be borne in mind when constructing this project. There is a very high gain from Tr1 base to Tr2 collector, and these two points are in-phase. Any stray feedback of significant proportions is therefore likely to cause instability, and reasonable care must be taken when designing the component layout. It is recommended that a metal case should be used for the unit, and that this should be earthed to the negative supply rail so that the circuit is screened from sources of electrical interference. Otherwise stray pick up at Tr1's base terminal may cause mains hum and other signals to be mixed into the white noise.

Resistors
R1   1.5M
R2   8.2k
R3   2.2M
R4   4.7k

Capacitors
C1   100 μF 10V
C2   1 μF 25V
C3   10 μF 25V

Semiconductors
Tr1   AF114 (see text)
Tr2   BC109C

Switch
S1   S.P.S.T.

Miscellaneous
Case, battery, battery connector, circuit board, wire, etc.

Pink Noise Generator

A white noise signal can be filtered to produce a pink noise signal using a filter having a response that has a roll off rate 10 dB per decade (i.e. increasing the input frequency by a factor of ten reduces the output to just under one third of its previous level). This filtering considerably attenuates the signal, and so amplification must be included in order to restore the signal to its previous level.

A simple white-to-pink noise converter is shown in the circuit diagram of Figure 17. Tr1 is basically connected as a conventional common emitter amplifier, but it has three C — R circuits connected between its base and collector terminals. These provide negative feedback over the amplifier, and the amount of feedback increases as the input frequency is increased, because the capacitors have an impedance that decreases with increasing frequency. The C — R values are chosen to give a frequency response that holds reasonably close to the required roll off rate. A single capacitor cannot be used to provide the equalisation incidentally, as this would produce an attenuation rate of double the required level. In effect C2 rolls off the response at the highest audio frequencies, and R2 prevents it from giving an excessive roll off rate. At middle frequencies C3 is primarily responsible for shaping the frequency response, and R3 suitably limits its effect. At low frequencies the response is mainly tailored by C4 and R4.

The full gain of Tr1 is not required, and so Tr1 is used to introduce a degree of attenuation. The input and output signal levels are then approximately equal. C1 and C5 are D.C. blocking capacitors at the input and output respectively. The current consumption of the circuit is only about 1 mA.

The circuit is extremely simple indeed, and even beginners should find construction of the unit perfectly straight forward. Note though, that as the low frequency gain of the circuit is considerably boosted by the addition of the white-to-pink noise unit, the susceptibility to stray pick up of mains hum is increased. It is really essential to house the circuitry in a metal case so that it is screened from sources of mains hum.

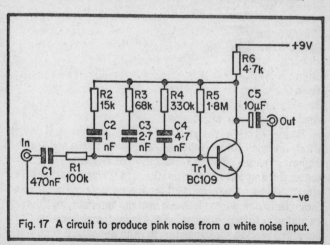

Fig. 17 A circuit to produce pink noise from a white noise input.

Although intended primarily for use with the white noise generator circuit of Figure 16, the circuit of Figure 17 can be used to process any white noise source having a similar output level.

Components Pink Noise Converter

Resistors
R1   100k
R2   15k
R3   68k
R4   330k
R5   1.8M
R6   4.7k

Capacitors
C1   470 nF plastic foil
C2   1 nF plastic foil
C3   2.7 nF plastic foil
C4   4.7 nF plastic foil
C5   10 μF 25V

Semiconductor
Tr1   BC109

Miscellaneous
Circuit board, wire, etc.

Tone Generator

An audio oscillator which covers a frequency range of about 50 Hz to 2 kHz (i.e. covers the normal range of musical notes) is extremely useful for producing electronic music and "science fiction" type sound effects. Melodies can be played by tuning the unit to the appropriate notes, giving a glissando effect. This simply means that the instruments output tone is varied from one note to another, rather than changing abruptly from one note to another. This effect can be obtained with many conventional instruments, such as violins and the other instruments of the violin family, where the player changes note by moving his or her finger up and down the fingerboard, rather than by normal fingering. Of course, this is an effect which cannot be obtained on many instruments of both the conventional and electronic varieties. It cannot be obtained on normal keyboard instruments for example. The glissando effect combines well with reverberation and echo effects to produce a rather weird and interesting overall effect.

The Circuit

The complete circuit diagram of the Tone Generator unit is shown in Figure 18, and this is basically just a 555 astable circuit. The timing components are R1, VR1, R2 and C1, VR1 acting as the tuning control. This gives an output frequency which is continuously variable from about 50 Hz at its maximum resistance setting, to 2 kHz at its minimum resistance one. This covers the musical notes from about the A which is the third one below middle C (55 Hz) to the B which is the third one above middle C (1.9755 kHz). The unit therefore covers a range of over 5 octaves. Note that VR1 is a logarithmic type, and not a linear component as one might have expected. The reason for using a logarithmic type is merely that this gives more even spacing of the notes. Using a linear component would result in the notes at the low frequency end of the scale being well spread out, at the expense of the higher notes being crammed into just a few degrees of rotation of VR1's shaft.

The output from pin 3 of IC1 is roughly a square wave. The mark space ratio is not actually precisely 1 to 1, and it does alter slightly with changes in the setting of VR1. This has little effect on the sound produced by the unit though, and for practical purposes the output can be regarded as a squarewave.

It is a simple matter to pass a square wave through simple filter networks to produce outputs of other shapes (and sounds), and two simple filters are incorporated in the unit for this purpose. The first of these is a single section C — R low pass filter which uses R3 and C4. This attenuates the higher

61

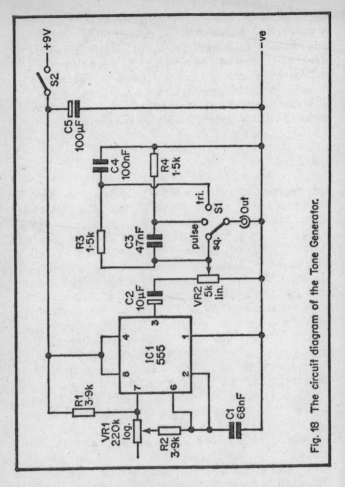

Fig. 18 The circuit diagram of the Tone Generator.

harmonics in the square wave signal, and produces a less harsh sounding output. The actual output waveform after this filtering is roughly triangular. The second filter is a single section C — R high pass type which is comprised of C3 and R4. This attenuates the fundamental signal to give a spikey, pulsed output, which has a very "bright" sound. The required output waveshape is selected by means of S1.

62

C2 provides D.C. blocking at the output, and VR2 is an output level control. The maximum output obtainable is about 8 volts peak to peak. C5 is a supply decoupling capacitor and S2 is the on/off switch. The circuit has a current consumption of about 8 mA.

This is another very simple project to construct, and the only point worth mentioning is that it is advisable to fit VR1 with a large control knob. This will make it easy to carry out the fine adjustments needed to tune the unit to the required note. A scale showing the positions of the various notes can be makred around the control knob of VR1, but it is unlikely that the unit could be tuned accurately enough by purely visual means. Using this type of equipment really requires a good ear for music and pitch, plus a little practice.

Components Tone Generator

Resistors
R1   3.9k
R2   3.9k
R3   1.5k
R4   1.5k
VR1   220k 1og. carbon
VR2   5k 1in. carbon

Capacitors
C1   68 nF plastic foil
C2   10 μF 10V
C3   47 nF plastic foil
C4   100 nF plastic foil
C5   100 μF 10V

Semiconductor
IC1   555

Switch
S1   S.P.S.T.

Miscellaneous
Case, circuit board, battery, battery connector, wire, etc.

Vibrato Oscillator

The output of the Tone Generator unit can, of course, be
processed by effects units to give more interesting sounds. It
is also possible to produce a good vibrato effect by applying a
low frequency signal into the previously unused pin 5 of IC1
in the tone generator circuit. The vibrato effect is produced
by frequency modulating the note produced by the unit. In
other words, a signal is used to vary the output frequency of
the unit up and down, giving a richer and more interesting
sound. The most pleasant vibrato effect is given using a
modulating frequency of a few Hz. Slower speeds tend to give
an effect which is not very noticeable, while higher modulating
speeds can easily produce rather harsh and unpleasant sounding
results. For best results only a low level of modulation is ·
required.

555 type astable circuits can easily be frequency modulated,
as the upper threshold voltage of this device can be varied by
means of a control voltage. As mentioned earlier, this control
voltage is applied to pin 5 of the device, which in most
applications is left unused. The upper threshold voltage of the
device is two thirds of the supply voltage, and the lower one
is one third of the supply voltage. 555 astable circuits operate
by having the timing capacitor first charged up to the higher
threshold voltage, and then when the circuit is triggered into
the discharge state, it discharges to the lower threshold voltage
through the I.C. and part of the timing resistance (that between
pins 6 and 7 of the device). The timing capacitor then charges
up to two thirds of the supply voltage again, the I.C. triggers to
the discharge state, the timing capacitor discharges to the
lower threshold voltage, and so on. This gives continuous
oscillation at a frequency determined by the timing components, and also by the threshold levels.

For example, if the upper threshold voltage is raised, it then
takes longer for the timing capacitor to charge up to this level,

and longer to discharge to the lower threshold potential, as the difference between the two threshold voltages is increased. This obviously reduces the operating frequency of the circuit. Reducing the upper threshold voltage has the opposite effect, as it reduces the difference between the two threshold levels, and the charge on the timing capacitor can vary between the two more frequently in a given period of time. This produces an increase in the operating frequency of the circuit. In this way the control voltage to pin 5 of the 555 gives the required frequency modulating effect.

The Circuit

The circuit diagram of a suitable vibrato oscillator for the tone generator unit appears in Figure 19. This uses a phase shift oscillator. Tr1 is used as a high gain common emitter amplifier having R3 as its base bias resistor and R4 as its collector load. Since the input (base) and output (collector) terminals of a common emitter amplifier are 180 degrees out-of-phase, a signal path between these two points will provide negative feedback and will not result in oscillation. Or to be more accurate, negative feedback will be produced unless the

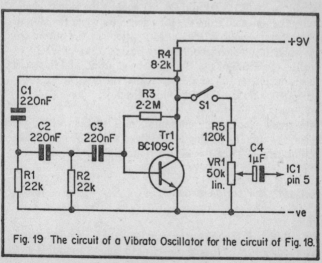

Fig. 19 The circuit of a Vibrato Oscillator for the circuit of Fig. 18.

feedback signal path introduces an inverting action. Positive feedback would then occur, and oscillation would result provided the losses through the feedback path are at least compensated for by the gain of the amplifier.

In this case the feedback path is provided by a three section phase shift network, and the three stages are comprised of C1 and R1, C2 and R2, and C3 plus the input impedance of the amplifier circuit. At a certain frequency there will be a 60 degree phase shift through each of the three networks, giving a total phase shift of the required 180 degrees. This results in positive feedback at this frequency, and as the gain of the amplifier amply compensates for the losses through the phase shift networks, the circuit oscillates at this frequency. A reasonably pure sine wave output is produced, and this gives a very smooth and pleasant vibrato effect. The values in the phase shift networks give an operating frequency of about 12 to 14 Hz, but the frequency can be changed, if desired, by altering the values of C1 to C3. The operating frequency is inversely proportional to the value of these capacitors, which should have the same value.

The output from the oscillator is coupled to the tone generator circuit by S1, R5, VR1 and C4. S1 enables the vibrato signal to be disconnected from the tone generator when the vibrato effect is not required. R5 is used to attenuate the output from the oscillator, which would otherwise be excessive. VR1 enables the depth of the vibrato to be adjusted, and in practice this is merely set to give the effect that the user finds most acceptable. C4 is a D.C. blocking capacitor.

The circuit has a current consumption of less than 1 mA. Once again, the circuit is so simple that there should be no complications whatever on the constructional side of things.

Components Vibrato Oscillator

Resistors
R1   22k
R2   22k

R3   2.2M
R4   8.2k
R5   120k
VR1   50k 1in. carbon

Capacitors
C1   220 nF plastic foil
C2   220 nF plastic foil
C3   220 nF plastic foil
C4   1 μF 25V

Semiconductor
Tr1   BC109C

Switch
S1   S.P.S.T.

Miscellaneous
Wire, circuit board, etc.

Stylus Organ

While a stylus organ does have limitations compared to one
having a proper keyboard, a great deal of fun can be had from
an instrument of this type. They are relatively simple and
inexpensive to construct, and can be made very compact as
well.

The main limitation of this type of instrument is that they are
only monophonic, which means that only one note at a time
can be played. Most keyboard instruments can produce a
number of notes simultaneously (polyphonic), and can thus
be used to play chords. However, the simplicity of stylus
organs does bring one big advantage, apart from ease of
construction and low cost: virtually anyone can learn to play
one in a fairly short time.

The instrument described here covers two octaves including
semitones (25 notes in all), the actual range covered being one
octave either side of the middle C. If preferred, the two

octaves above middle C can be covered, and this merely entails changing C5 from 47 nf to 22 nf and tuning the instrument accordingly. The circuit includes a vibrato oscillator which considerably enhances the sound of the instrument when switched into action.

The Circuit

Figure 20 shows the complete circuit diagram of the Stylus Organ. The tone generator uses a relaxation oscillator based on unijunction transistor Tr2. A unijunction device has little in common with an ordinary bipolar transistor. Two of its three terminals are bases, and these are normally called base 1 and base 2 so that they can be distinguished from one another. There is a resistance of a few kilohms between these two terminals under quiescent conditions. The third terminal is called the emitter, and if it is suitably forward biased, the resistance between the two base terminals falls to only about half its normal level, and the normally high emitter input impedance falls to a low level. It is this effect that enables a unijunction transistor to be used in a relaxation oscillator circuit.

The base 2 and base 1 terminals of unijunction device Tr2 are connected to the positive and negative supplies respectively by R7 and R8. The emitter terminal is connected to the positive supply via R6 and whichever of the twenty five tuning resistances is selected using the stylus. C5 is connected from this terminal to the negative supply, and so Tr2's emitter will be at earth potential when the unit is first switched on. C5 will rapidly charge up by way of the tuning resistance though, giving an increasing forward bias to the emitter of Tr2 as it does so. When the charge on C5 reaches about 80% of the supply potential, the forward bias on Tr2 will be sufficient to trigger the device into its low resistance state. The current through the base 1 and base 2 terminals then increases substantially due to the fall in resistance across these two points. Of course, this also causes the current through R7 and R8 to rise, generating a rise in voltage across both components.

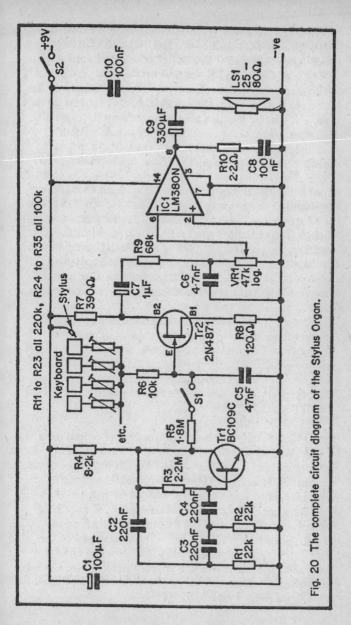

Fig. 20 The complete circuit diagram of the Stylus Organ.

69

C5 now rapidly discharges due to the drop in the input impedance to Tr2's emitter terminal. When C5 has largely discharged, the forward bias on Tr2 is no longer sufficient to hold the device in the low resistance state, and it reverts back to its original condition. The voltages across R7 and R8 then return to their previous levels, and C5 starts to charge up once again. It quickly attains a high enough charge to trigger Tr2, and the whole process thus continuously repeats itself, producing the required oscillation. The output signal is the stream of brief negative pulses that are produced across R7.

The twenty five timing resistances are adjusted so that they produced the appropriate range of notes. R11 to R23 (220k in value) give the notes from middle C downwards, and R24 to R35 (100k in value) give the notes above middle C. The oscillator circuit is very stable and is not significantly affected by variations in supply voltage and ambient temperature. Once correctly tuned, it therefore stays in tune for a considerable length of time, and will rarely, if ever, need retuning.

The output from the tone generator is coupled by C7 and R9 to the volume control, VR1. R9 is used to attenuate the output from Tr2, which is otherwise somewhat higher than is really needed. It also forms a top cut filter in conjunction with C6. This attenuates the higher frequency harmonics on the output from the tone generator, and gives a more musical sound from the instrument.

An LM380N audio I.C. is used to amplify the output from the volume control to a high enough level to drive a high impedance loudspeaker at good volume. The LM380N has both inverting (-) and non-inverting (+) inputs, and in this circuit the input signal is applied to the former, while the latter is earthed so that stray feedback cannot cause instability. The inverting input is directly connected to the volume control, and no D.C. blocking capacitor is needed here. The voltage gain of the LM380N is set at a nominal level of 50 times (34 dB) by an internal negative feedback circuit. R10 and C8 form a Zobel network, and aid the stability of the circuit. C9 provides D.C. blocking at the output.

A maximum output power of between about 100 and 300 mW
is available, depending upon the speaker impedance used.
Lower impedance types give the highest output power, but
there should be perfectly adequate volume even if an 80
ohm type is used. It is recommended that speakers of less than
25 ohms impedance should not be used.

The vibrato oscillator is a phase shift type, and it is basically
identical to the one shown in Figure 19, and described earlier.
It will not, therefore, be described again here. Its output is
coupled by R5 and S1 to the emitter terminal of Tr2. When the
output from the oscillator is positive going, a current flows
through R4 and R5 into timing capacitor C5, and this obviously
decreases the charge time of C5, producing a consequent rise
in the tone generator's frequency. When the vibrato oscillator's
output is negative going, some of the charge current to C5 is
diverted through R5 and the base — emitter terminals of
Tr1, causing a rise in the charge time of C5 and a subsequent
decrease in the operating frequency of the tone generator. Thus
the frequency modulation of the vibrato effect is achieved.
S1 can be used to switch off the vibrato when it is not required.

C1 and C10 are both supply decoupling capacitors, and C10
should be positioned as physically close to IC1 as possible. S2
is the on/off switch. As the LM380N device has a class B output stage, the current consumption of the unit varies to a
considerable extent with changes in the volume control setting.
At low volume levels and under quiescent conditions the
current drain is typically about 10 mA or so, but it can rise to
more than 50 mA at high volume settings. It is therefore
recommended that a fairly large 9 volt battery, such as a PP7
or PP9 size, should be used to power the instrument.

The main difficulty regarding the construction of this project is
producing the keyboard contacts. Probably the best method is
to use a printed circuit keyboard, designed with the contacts
in the normal piano type keyboard arrangement so that the
notes can be readily identified. However, there are alternative
methods, and large panel head screws can be used to provide the
contacts. These can have soldertags fitted on the underside to
provide connection points for the present tuning resistors. The

71

screws can be arranged in the conventional piano type keyboard arrangement to ease the identification of the various notes. No doubt there are many other alternative methods, and it is really just a matter of using ones initiative here.

If a p.c.b. type keyboard is used, it would be logical to design the p.c.b. to take the tuning presets as well, although it may well be more convenient to use a separate board for the remaining circuitry. If some other form of keyboard is used it will probably be best to mount the presets on the underside of the contacts if possible, or failing that they can be fairly easily wired up on a piece of plain matrix or stripboard. However, this would necessitate twenty five connecting wires between the preset panel and the contacts. It is advisable to use standard size (0.25W) rather than subminature presets (0.1W) as the larger types give more precise and easier tuning. They do, unfortunately, require a comparitively large amount of space though, and if a miniature instrument is to be made it will almost certainly be necessary to use subminiature types. Multiturn types are ideal, but unless inexpensive surplus types can be obtained the cost of these would be prohibitively expensive.

The instrument is tuned "by ear", using another musical instrument that is correctly tuned to provide the reference notes. Alternatively, a set of pitch pipes can be used to provide the reference notes. It is just a matter of adjusting each preset to produce the appropriate note, and it is advisable to do this methodically so as to avoid confusion and errors.

Finally, for those who are unfamiliar with the arrangement of piano type keyboards, Figure 21 should help to clarify matters.

Components Stylus Organ

Resistors
R1   22k
R2   22k
R3   2.2M
R4   8.2k

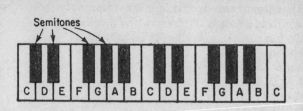

Fig. 21 The arrangement of a piano-type keyboard
(two octaves, C to C).

R5   1.8M
R6   10k
R7   390 ohms
R8   120 ohms
R9   68k
R10   2.2 ohms
R11 to R23   220k 0.1 watt presets (13 off)
R24 to R25   100k 0.1 watt presets (12 off)
VR1   47k 1og. carbon

Capacitors
C1   100 μF 10V
C2   220 nF plastic foil
C3   220 nF plastic foil
C4   220 nF plastic foil
C5   47 nF plastic foil
C6   4.7 nF plastic foil
C7   1 μF 25V
C8   100 nF plastic foil
C9   330 μF 10V
C10   100 nF plastic foil

Semiconductors
IC1   LM380N
Tr1   BC109C
Tr2   2N4871

Loudspeaker
LS1   Miniature speaker having an impedance in range
      25 to 80 ohms

Switches
S1   S.P.S.T.
S2   S.P.S.T.

Miscellaneous
Case, materials for keyboard (see text), circuit board, stylus
(test prod, jack plug, etc.), battery, battery connector, wire
speaker fret, etc.

CHAPTER 4

ACCESSORIES

There are a large number of electronic projects which are
connected in some way with music, although not actually
being used to produce sounds or effects. This final chapter
will describe a selection of these musical accessories, including
such projects as a metronome, tuning reference, and a guitar
practice amplifier.

Guitar Tuning Fork

The purpose of this device is to generate the six open string
notes of a guitar, to assist with tuning. It is an electronic
version of conventional pitch pipes or tuning forks in fact. The
complete circuit diagram of the unit is shown in Figure 22.

It is obviously important for the tone generator circuit to be
extremely stable so that once the unit has initially been tuned
and set up, no further adjustment will be required for a considerable length of time, otherwise the unit would be pointless.
An ordinary R — C oscillator is capable of providing perfectly
adequate stability, but only if it is a type which has an output
frequency that is virtually independant of the supply voltage,
or a well stabilised supply is used. It should be borne in mind
that the unit must be portable, and therefore battery powered.
The voltage provided by a normal dry cell varies by about 25
to 30% during its normal lifespan, and so a supply voltage
conscious oscillator would not give good results unless a
regulator were to be included in the design.

A simple 555 astable type circuit is used to generate the six
tones, and despite the simplicity of this configuration, it is very
stable and obviates the need for any supply stabilisation. This
type of circuit is inherently stable, since although, say, a rise in
supply voltage would increase the rate at which the timing
capacitor was charged, the two threshold voltages would also

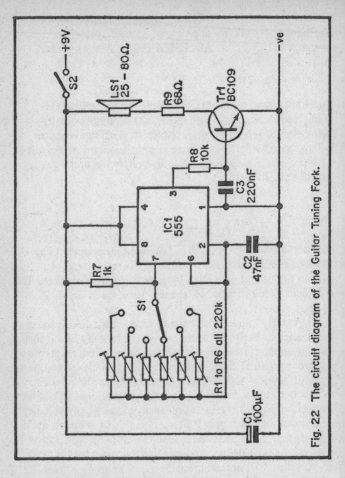

Fig. 22 The circuit diagram of the Guitar Tuning Fork.

increase in value (still remaining at one third and two thirds of the supply potential). Thus the rise in the charge rate would be cancelled out by the rise in the difference between the two threshold voltages, theoretically preventing any change in operating frequency. In practice there is likely to be some small variation in output frequency with changes in the supply voltage, but this will be far too small to be of any consequence in this application.

The timing components of the oscillator are R7, C2 and whichever of the six preset resistors (R1 to R6) is selected using S1. Each preset is adjusted to give a different guitar note, so that all six notes (E, A, D, G, B, E) are available from the unit.

The output from pin 3 of IC1 is fed to the base of common emitter amplifier transistor, Tr1, via current limiting resistor R8. LS1 and current limiting resistor R9 form the collector load for TR1. When the output from IC1 is high, Tr1 is biased hard into conduction and a strong current is fed to the loud-speaker. When the output from IC1 is low, Tr1 is cut off and no significant current is fed to the speaker. Thus the speaker is fed with a series of current pulses, and an audio tone is produced. The output waveshape is roughly square, and is therefore rich in harmonics. C3 provides top cut filtering in conjunction with R8, attenuating the harmonics and making the fundamental frequency more prominent. In practice this makes the unit a little easier to use.

C1 is a supply decoupling capacitor and S2 is an ordinary on/off switch. The current consumption of the unit is approximately 40 mA, but varies to some extent with speaker impedance and output frequency. As the unit is only likely to be used for short periods it should be found that even a small 9 volt battery, such as a PP3 size one, gives economic operation.

There should be no problems with the construction of the project. The six output tones are tuned "by ear" against a guitar that is correctly tuned, pitch pipes, or any musical instrument that is in tune and provides the appropriate notes.

Components Guitar Tuning Fork

Resistors
R1 to R6   220k 0.25 watt presets (6 off)
R7   1k.
R8   10k
R9   68 ohms

Capacitors
C1   100 μF 10V
C2   47 nF plastic foil
C3   220 nF plastic foil

Semiconductors
IC1   555
Tr1   BC109

Switches
S1   6 way 2 pole rotary (only one pole used).
S2   S.P.S.T.

Loudspeaker
LS1   Miniature type having an impedance in the range 25 to
         80 ohms

Miscellaneous
Case, component board, 9 volt battery, connector to suit, wire,
etc.

Guitar Practice Amplifier

This simple and inexpensive amplifier is ideal for guitar practice
at home, where powerful commercial units may be incon-
veniently large and loud. A particularly useful feature of the
amplifier is the provision of a phones socket, which permits
personal listening and avoids annoyance to others when
practicing. The output power of the unit depends upon the
impedance of the speaker that is employed with it, with about
100 mW R.M.S. being obtainable with an 80 ohm type, rising
to about 1 watt R.M.S. with an 8 ohm speaker (probably
somewhat less in practice due to the internal resistance of the
battery causing a significant drop in the supply voltage at high
output powers). The circuit diagram is shown in Figure 23.

The output stage uses an LM380N I.C. in the inverting mode,
the non-inverting (+) input being connected to earth in order to
prevent possible stray positive feedback, and consequent
instability. The output from IC1 is coupled to the loudspeaker

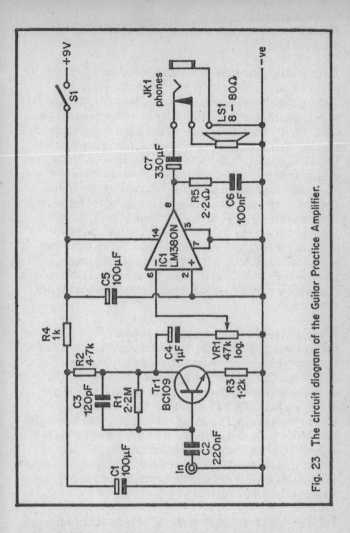

Fig. 23 The circuit diagram of the Guitar Practice Amplifier.

via D.C. blocking capacitor C7 and a break contact on phones jack, JK1. This break contact automatically switches off the loudspeaker when the headphones are plugged into JK1. R5

and C6 form a Zobel network, and are needed in order to aid the stability of IC1. The inverting input connects direct to the

79

slider of volume control, VR1, and no D.C. blocking capacitor is needed here.

An internal negative feedback network sets the voltage gain of IC1 at a nominal figure of 34 dB (50 times). This is not quite sufficient for the present application, and a preamplifier stage is therefore added ahead of the power amplifier. This has Tr1 in the common emitter mode, but it does not provide the high level of voltage gain that one normally expects from this configuration. This is due to the inclusion of the unbypassed emitter resistor, R3, which introduces a considerable amount of negative feedback to this stage. The voltage gain of the preamplifier is approximately equal to R2 divided by R3, or a little less than 12 dB (4 times) in other words. This raises the sensitivity of the unit sufficiently, and gives an input sensitivity of about 15 mV R.M.S. into 250k for maximum output power. C3 rolls off the response of the preamplifier above about 20 kHz, and this aids the stability of the amplifier. It also helps to eliminate R.F. breakthrough and consequent interference.

It is important for the preamplifier to be well decoupled from the power amplifier in order to prevent stray feedback through the supply lines. Appropriate supply decoupling is given by C1, R4 and C5. On/off switching is provided by S1. The quiescent current consumption of the circuit is typically about 9 mA, but the LM380N has a class B output stage and the current drain is therefore considerably higher than this at high volume levels. In fact, at high volume levels when using an 8 ohm speaker, the average current consumption can exceed 100 mA. It is advisable to power the unit from a fairly large 9 volt battery, such as PP7 or PP9, especially if a low impedance speaker is used with the unit.

Construction of the amplifier should be quite straight forward, but the layout of the circuit is obviously fairly critical due to the quite high gain and input impedance of the unit. Reasonable care must be taken to ensure that no strong feedback paths from the output to the input are produced. Also, care must be taken to avoid earth loops. Either of these could cause instability if they should be allowed to occur.

The amplifier should work perfectly well using low, medium, or high impedance headphones plugged into JK1. Low, medium, and high impedance magnetic earphones are also as suitable match for the amplifier, as are a crystal earphone or headphones.

Components Guitar Practice Amplifier

Resistors
R1   2.2M
R2   4.7k
R3   1.2k
R4   1k
R5   2.2 ohms
VR1 47k log. carbon

Capacitors
C1   100 μF 10V
C2   220 nF plastic foil
C3   120 pF ceramic plate
C4   1 μF 25V
C5   100 μF 10V
C6   100 nF plastic foil
C7   330 μF 10V

Semiconductors
IC1 LM380N
Tr1 BC109

Switch
S1   S.P.S.T.

Socket
JK1 3.5 mm. jack socket with single break contact

Loudspeaker
LS1 Any type having an impedance in the range 8 to 80 ohms

Miscellaneous
Case, circuit board, 9 volt battery, battery connector, wire, etc.

Metronome

A conventional metronome (Maelzel's metronome) produces a
regular "clicking" sound by mechanical means, and helps
players to play pieces at the correct speed. Many pieces of
music are marked with the required number of beats per
minute, and by setting the metronome at the appropriate rate,
the "clicks" it produces will indicate the correct speed for the
piece.

There have been many designs for electronic metronomes which
simulate the sound of a conventional metronome, but many of
these overlook the visual indication provided by the conventional
instrument. It has an arm which swings from side to side,
giving the visual indication of the tempo. It is, of course, quite
simple to design an electronic metronome that will give a visual
indication as well as an audible one, the obvious solution being
to include an indicator light which flashes on at the same time
as each "click" is produced.

It is a simple metronome of this type which is featured here,
and its circuit diagram appears in Figure 24. A 555 astable
circuit is used to provide the pulses needed to operate the
loudspeaker and indicator light. The pulses only need to be
quite brief in order to produce the "clicking" sound which is
quite high pitched and should contain very little in the way of
bass frequencies. R2 has therefore been given a low value in
comparison to the other section of the timing resistance (R1
plus VR1) so as to give the brief (negative) output pulses. This
occurs because C2 charges through R1, VR1 and R2 (output
high), but only discharges through R2 plus the very low
impedance presented by IC1 (output low). This obviously
results in the discharge time being far shorter than the charge
time, giving the short negative pulses at the output.

VR1 controls the operating frequency, and gives an operating
range of about 35 to 350 beats per minute. It is recommended
that timing capacitor C2 should be a non-electrolytic type as
these have far lower tolerances than most electrolytic components. The tolerance of the capacitor is still likely to be
10 or 20%, and that of VR1 will almost certainly be 20%, so

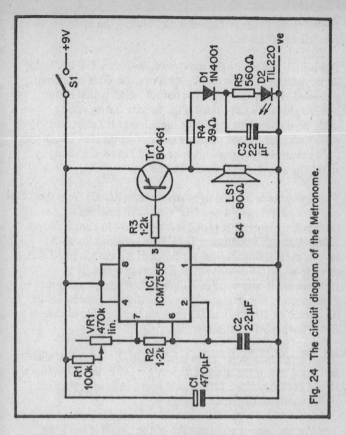

Fig. 24 The circuit diagram of the Metronome.

that the frequency range of the unit cannot be predicted with a high degree of accuracy. However, the nominal range of the circuit has purposely been made slightly larger than really necessary so that even with inaccuracies in the timing component values the unit should still cover all the wanted beat rates.

IC1 drives common emitter amplifier, Tr1, via current limiting resistor R3. The loudspeaker forms the main collector load for Tr1. For most of the time IC1's output is high, and Tr1 is cut off. It is biased hard into conduction during the brief negative excursions at IC1's output producing short bursts of

83

current through the loudspeaker and causing the metronome-like "clicking" sounds.

The L.E.D. indicator light could be driven from Tr1's collector by way of the usual current limiting resistor. This would not give good results though, as the output pulses would be too brief to give a clear signal from the L.E.D. Better results could be obtained by increasing the value of R2 so as to produce longer output pulses. This would pulse the L.E.D. on for a longer time, giving a brighter flash, but would adversely affect the sound output from the unit.

This is overcome by feeding reservoir capacitor C3 from the collector of Tr1 via R4 and D1. When Tr1 switches on, the brief pulse of current it provides is sufficient to almost fully charge C3. L.E.D. indicator D2 is then powered from C3 by way of current limiting resistor R5 until the charge on C3 dies away to an insufficient level. It does so very rapidly in fact, but D2 is held on slightly longer than the output pulse duration, and this produces a very worthwhile increase in the brightness of the flashes. D1 prevents any significant charge from flowing off C3 through LS1.

"High brightness" and "extra bright" L.E.D.s are now available, and using one of these high efficiency types in the D2 position would probably give a further and worthwhile improvement in the clarity of the visual indication.

The average current consumption of the circuit is less than 2 mA. The circuit can therefore be economically powered by a small 9 volt battery, such as a PP3 size one. During the output pulses the current consumption peaks at several hundred mA, and a high value supply decoupling capacitor (C1) is therefore needed in order to help supply these high bursts of current. S1 is an ordinary on/off switch.

Construction of the unit should be fairly easy and straight forward. It is advisable to fit a large pointer knob to VR1 so that an accurate calibrated scale can be marked arount it. The beat rate is found merely by counting the number of clicks produced in a one minute period (or, say, in a 20 second period, and multiplying by three). Rub-on transfers can be used to give a neat and professional looking finish to the scale.

Components Metronome

Resistors
R1   100k
R2   1.2k
R3   1.2k
R4   39 ohms
R5   560 ohms
VR1 470k 1in. carbon

Capacitors
C1   470 μF 10V
C2   2.2 μF plastic foil
C3   22 μF 10V

Semiconductors
IC1   ICM7555
Tr1   BC461
D1   1N4001
D2   TIL220, etc., with panel clip

Switch
S1   S.P.S.T.

Loudspeaker
LS1   Miniature type having an impedance in the range 64 to 80 ohms.

Miscellaneous
Case, circuit board, 9 volt battery, battery connector, etc.

Automatic Fader

An automatic fader is used to gradually and smoothly fade out a signal, without introducing any noise spikes or other noises, simply by operating a switch. Most circuits of this type, including the one described here, have the ability to "fade" the signal back up to full level, also by merely operating a switch. Units of this type can be used in a number of fields, including the production of electronic music, tapes to accompany slide or cine shows, and at discos. The circuit diagram appears in Figure 25.

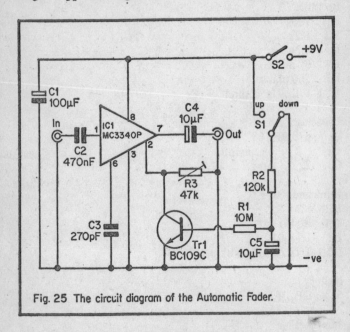

Fig. 25 The circuit diagram of the Automatic Fader.

The circuit is based on the MC3340P electronic attenuator I.C. The input signal is coupled into the attenuator device by C2, and is extracted from the output terminal via D.C. blocking capacitor, C4. C3 rolls off the response of the circuit at high frequencies, aiding the stability of the circuit.

The gain of IC1 is controlled by the collector to emitter resistance of Tr1. When Tr1 is biased to conduct reasonably strongly, IC1 exhibits its full voltage gain of about 13 dB (a little over four times). This reduces to an attenuation of about 70 or 80 dB. when Tr1 is cut off, or is barely in a state of conduction.

Initially S1 is in the "down" position, and C5 is totally un-charged. No base bias is supplied to Tr1, which is cut off in consequence. The signal is therefore severely attenuated as it passes through the circuit, and for all practical purposes it can be regarded as being completely blocked by the unit.

If S1 is switched to the "up" position, over the course of a few seconds C5 will charge up by way of R2. As the voltage across C5 increases, Tr1 becomes increasingly forward biased by the base current received through R1.. When C5 becomes almost fully charged, Tr1 will be biased sufficiently to cause IC1 to operate at maximum gain.

Thus, the input signal is initially blocked, but is brought up to maximum level over a period of a few seconds when S1 is operated, giving a "fade in" effect. If S1 is then returned to the "down" position, R2 discharges C5 over a period of a few seconds. This results in Tr1 gradually switching off, and the gain of IC1 returning to its former level. This gives a smooth "fade out" effect.

It has been assumed in this explanation that R3 is set at maximum resistance, and places a resistance into circuit that is too high to have any significant effect on the gain of IC1. If a maximum fade out level of less than the -70 to 80 dB provided by the basic circuit is required, R3 can be adjusted to limit the maximum attenuation of IC1 to the required level. R3 can be omitted if the highest possible fade out level will always be required, as may well be the case in many applications.

C1 provides supply decoupling and S2 is the on/off switch. The current consumption of the circuit is approximately 6 to 7 mA. The input impedance of the circuit is about 50k and input voltages of up to 500 mV R.M.S. can be handled without the output becoming clipped. The T.H.D. (total harmonic distortion) figure is typically below 1% except at higher attenuation levels where it rises to 2 or 3%. This is more than adequate for the majority of applications.

The specified timing component values give "fade in" and "fade out" times of about two seconds or so in each case. This can be altered, if required, by changing the value of C5. The fade times are roughly proportional to the value of this capacitor.

Components Automatic Fader

Resistors
R1   10M
R2   120k
R3   47k 0.1 watt preset

Capacitors
C1   100 μF 10V
C2   470 nF plastic foil
C3   270 pF ceramic plate
C4   10 μF 25V
C5   10 μF 25V

Semiconductors
IC1   MC3340P
Tr1   BC109C

Switches
S1   S.P.D.T.
S2   S.P.S.T.

Miscellaneous
Case, circuit board, 9 volt battery, battery connector, wire, etc.

Voice Operated Fader

The purpose of a voice operated fader is to mix a voice signal and a music signal, and to also fade out the music signal automatically when the voice signal is present. Units of this type are mainly used at discos, and in the production of tapes to accompany slide and cine shows. They can also be used in the production of electronic music, where the two inputs might be from (say) a noise generator and a tone generator, rather than a voice and a music source. The circuit diagram is given in Figure 26.

The music signal (or other controlled signal) is coupled by C3 to the input of an MC3340P electronic attenuator device, IC1. The output from this is coupled by C6 to the input of a conventional two channel mixer circuit. The control input is coupled direct to the other input of the mixer circuit.

The control signal is also taken to the input of a common emitter amplifier which is based on Tr1. C1 provides input D.C. blocking, R1 is the base bias resistor, and R2 is the collector load resistor. The unbypassed emitter resistor, R3, introduces a controlled amount of negative feedback to this stage, and by adjusting R3 it is possible to vary the voltage gain from a little under 6 dB (2 times) to almost 40 dB (100 times).

C2 couples the output from Tr1 to a rectifier and smoothing network which is comprised of D1, D2 and C4. The quiescent gain of IC1 is set at approximately unity by R4. In the presence of a suitably strong signal at the control input though, a strong positive bias will be generated by the smoothing and rectifier circuitry. This takes the control input of IC1 more positive, causing a loss of gain through the device and fading out the controlled signal. Thus the required automatic fade out action is obtained. The circuit can produce a strong enough bias to produce the maximum available attenuation from the MC3340P, which is some 75 to 80 dB.

The attack time of the circuit is made quite short (a few mS) so that the controlled signal is faded out almost as soon as the control signal is introduced, but the attack time is not so short as to introduce "clicks" or other noises as the fade out occurs. The decay time is a little longer, although still quite short, giving a smooth "fade in" that is not too abrupt. If desired, a longer "fade in" time can be obtained by increasing the value of C4, but this component should not be made too high in value, as this would result in the attack time of the circuit being excessive for most applications.

A conventional operational amplifier based mixer circuit

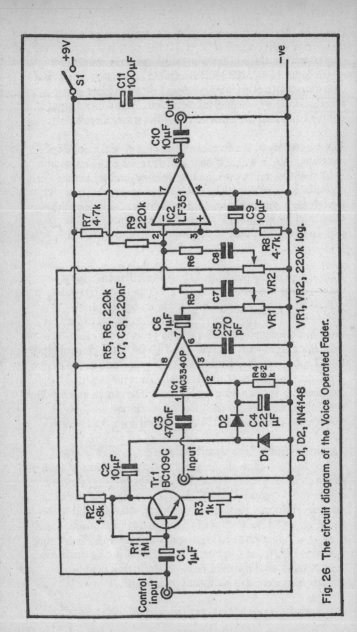

Fig. 26 The circuit diagram of the Voice Operated Fader.

90

is used to combine the control and controlled signals, this stage being built around IC2. IC2 is basically just an inverting amplifier, with the non-inverting input biased to half the supply potential by R7 and R8. C9 decouples this input from any noise on the supply lines. The negative feedback loop has two input resistors (R5 and R6) so that the two input signals can be coupled independantly into the amplifier, one input being applied to each resistor. There is the normal single feedback resistor between the output and inverting input of the operational amplifier (R9), and as this has the same value as R5 and R6, there is a voltage gain of approximately unity from each input to the output. The circuit responds to the sum of the two input voltages, giving the required adding, or mixing action at the output. Isolation is provided between the two inputs as what is called a "virtual earth" is formed at the inverting input of IC2. In simple terms, this means that the negative feedback action stabilises the voltage at the inverting input at a fixed level (the same potential as appears at the non-inverting input). Since there is a constant voltage here, there is no signal path from one input to the other.

On/off switching is provided by S1, and C11 is the only supply decoupling capacitor that is needed. The current consumption of the circuit is approximately 10 mA, and this can be economically provided by a medium sized 9 volt battery, such as a PP6 type (or equivalent).

R3 is given the highest resistance setting that gives reliable operation of the circuit. Adjusting it for a higher level of gain than is really necessary could result in unwanted operations of the fader circuitry, and should therefore be avoided. If it is only necessary for the controlled signal to be partially faded out, as will probably be the case in most applications, by adjusting R3 it should be possible to obtain the required level of fade out. The unit will function correctly with input levels to the controlled input over a wide range of about 20 mV to 2 volts R.M.S.

Resistors
R1   1M
R2   1.8k
R3   1k 0.1 watt preset
R4   8.2k
R5   220k
R6   220k
R7   4.7k
R8   4.7k
R9   220k
VR1 220k log. carbon
VR2 220k log. carbon

Capacitors
C1   1 μF 25V
C2   10 μF 25V
C3   470 nF plastic foil
C4   22 μF 10V
C5   270 pF ceramic plate
C6   1 μF 25V
C7   220 nF plastic foil
C8   220 nF plastic foil
C9   10 μF 25V
C10 10 μF 25V
C11 100 μF 10V

Semiconductors
IC1 MC3340P
IC2 LF351
Tr1 1N4148
D2   1N4148

Switch
S1   S.P.S.T.

Miscellaneous
Case, circuit board, 9 volt battery, battery connector, wire, etc.

Simple Mixer

A mixer is an extremely useful piece of equipment for anyone interested in electronic music to have; it could even be considered an essential item of equipment. It can be used to enable a number of guitars or other instruments to feed into a single amplifier, or it can be used in the production of electronic music tapes. Mixers are also used in disco equipment, and in many other applications.

The mixer described here has a very simple circuit (Figure 27), but is nevertheless very useful and versatile, and achieves quite a high level of performance. The circuit utilizes an operational amplifier (IC1), and is basically the same as the mixer used in the "Voice Operated Fader" unit which was described in the previous section of this book. The two main differences are the addition of an extra input resistor, plus its associated D.C. blocking capacitor and level control, so that there are three inputs. In fact, any number of inputs can be obtained by adding the appropriate number of input resistors and their associated components. The other main difference is that feedback resistor R6 has been given a higher value, so that the circuit can provide a small amount of voltage gain (about 7 dB, or a little over two times in other words).

There are two useful additions at the output of the circuit. The first is an output level control, VR4, which effectively enables the levels of all three channels to be varied simultaneously. The other, and more major addition, is a peak level indicator, and while a VU (volume units) meter is ideal, it would substantially add to the cost of the project. A peak level indicator has the advantage of being cheap and simple to install, and gives a visual warning if the output exceeds some predetermined level.

The peak level indicator uses Tr1 as an unbiased common emitter amplifier. L.E.D. indicator D2 and current limiting resistor R8 form its collector load. On input signals to the base of Tr1 of less than about 1.2V peak to peak, positive going half cycles will be insufficient to switch on Tr1. Signals above this level will switch on Tr1 during peak positive

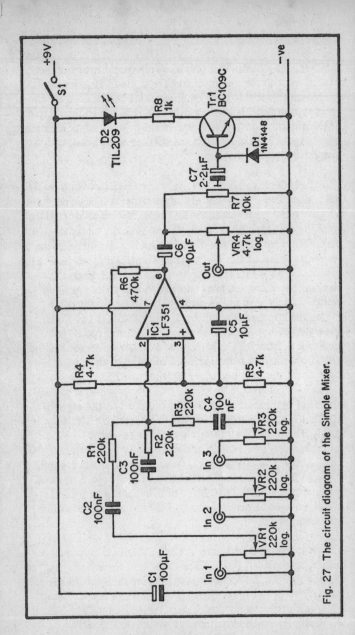

Fig. 27 The circuit diagram of the Simple Mixer.

excursions, causing D2 to visibly glow and indicate that the
threshold level has been exceeded. D1 is needed to ensure that
the input signal to Tr1's base swings symetrically either side of
the negative supply rail. Without D1 the base of Tr1 would
tend to go negative of the negative supply rail, and inputs of
several volts peak to peak would fail to switch on Tr1. R7 can
be used to adjust the threshold level at which D2 switches on,
and thresholds of between about 400 mV and 2V R.M.S. can
be obtained.

The on/off switch is S1 and supply decoupling is provided by
C1. The current consumption of the circuit is about 2 mA,
although this can increase by a few mA when D2 is operating.
A small 9 volt battery such as a PP3 size can therefore be used
to power the project. The input impedance at each input of the
unit is over 100k, which is high enough to ensure minimal
loading on items of equipment used to feed the unit. Signals of
up to about 2.5V R.M.S. can be handled without the output
becoming clipped. A higher overload margin can be obtained
by using two 9 volt batteries in series to power the unit, so as to
obtain an 18 volt supply (C1 must then be changed to a 25
volt type). The unit has a very low noise level, and it will
therefore give a reasonable performance in this respect if it is
used to process low level signals, say from a guitar. It is not
really suitable for use with very low level signals, such as those
obtained from a low impedance dynamic microphone, and a
suitable preamplifier should then be added at the input in
order to obtain really good results.

Components Simple Mixer

Resistors
R1   220k
R2   220k
R3   220k
R4   4.7k
R5   4.7k
R6   470k
R7   10k 0.1 watt preset
R8   1k

95

VR1 220k log. carbon
VR2 220k log. carbon
VR3 220k log. carbon
VR4 4.7k log. carbon

Capacitors
C1 100 μF 25V
C2 100 nF plastic foil
C3 100 nF plastic foil
C4 100 nF plastic foil
C5 10 μF 25V
C6 10 μF 25V
C7 2.2 μF 25V

Semiconductors
IC1 LF351
Tr1 BC109C
D1 1N4148
D2 TIL209

Switch
S1 S.P.S.T.

Miscellaneous
Case, circuit board, 9 volt battery, battery connector, wire, etc.

Sound To Light Unit

The majority of "pop" groups and discos these days are
equipped with some form of lighting effects unit(s); the most
common ones being sound to light units, stobe units, and
colour wheels. The circuit described here is for a very simple
and inexpensive sound to light unit which gives a very
effective display. The basic idea of the unit is to provide a
"moving lights" type display, where the speed of the display
varies in sympathy with volume of the music. The louder the
music, the faster the operating speed of the unit.

The circuit diagram of the clock oscillator section of the unit
is shown in Figure 28. The purpose of this part of the unit is

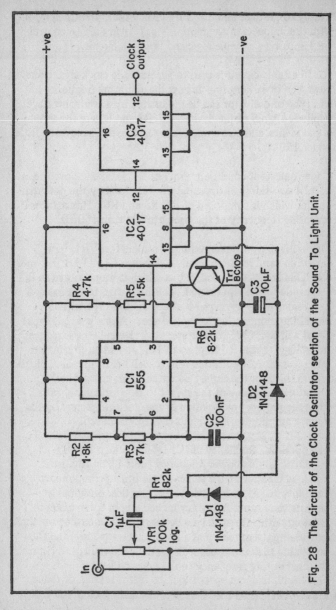

Fig. 28 The circuit of the Clock Oscillator section of the Sound To Light Unit.

97

merely to produce an output frequency that varies in sympathy with the loudness of the music. This is then used to control the lamps via a suitable logic and isolation circuit.

A 555 astable circuit is used to generate the clock signal, and we have seen in earlier projects how the operating frequency of this type of oscillator can be modulated by a control voltage applied to pin 5 of the device. R2, R3 and C2 are the timing components, and give a nominal operating frequency of a little under 150 Hz.

Under quiescent conditions pin 5 of IC1 is taken above the normal two thirds of the supply voltage level by the potential divider which is comprised of R4, R5 and R6. This reduces the operating frequency of the circuit to less than 100 Hz.

The input signal is taken via input attenuator, VR1, to a smoothing and rectifier circuit which uses C1, R1 D1, D2 and C3. This produces a positive bias which is proportional to the amplitude of the input signal. This bias is fed to the base of Tr1, and if the input signal is strong enough, Tr1 will be biased into conduction to some degree. A really strong input signal will cause Tr1 to saturate. As Tr1 conducts, it reduces the voltage that is fed to pin 5 of IC1, and when it is biased into saturation, it pulls this voltage well below its normal level of two thirds of the supply potential. This causes the operating frequency of the circuit to be considerably raised. Thus the required modulation of the clock frequency by the average amplitude of the input signal is produced.

The operating frequency of IC1 is far too high for this application, and a lower frequency could obviously be obtained by altering the values of the timing components. This does not seem to work well in practice, presumably because the output frequency is then low in comparison to the modulating frequencies. Better results seem to be obtained by running the oscillator at a fairly high frequency, and then processing the output using digital divider circuitry to reduce the final output frequency to the required level.

This is the method used here, and the frequency division is

provided by IC2 and IC3. These are both CMOS 4017 devices which are decade counters and one of ten decoders. In this circuit they are only used as decade counters, giving a total frequency division factor of 100. This gives an output frequency in the region of 1 Hz. If desired, the nominal output frequency can be changed to some extent by altering the value of C2. The output frequency is inversely proportional to the value of this component.

Logic Circuitry

The logic circuitry of the unit is shown in Figure 29. This is based on another 4017 device, and this time it is used as a form of one of ten decoder, although in actual fact most of these ten outputs are unused. As its name suggests, a one of ten decoder has ten outputs, and one of these is in the high logic state while the others are in the low state. The outputs are numbered "0" to "9", and initially the "0" output is the one that is in the high state. On successive clock pulses, outputs "1" to "9" go high in sequence, and then the devices cycles back to output "0" in the high state, whereupon the sequence of operation starts once again from the beginning.

In this case, after outputs "0", "1" and "2" have gone high, the circuit cycles straight back to the "0" output high state, with outputs "4" to "9" never going high. This is because the "3" output (pin 7) is connected to the reset input (pin 15), and so the circuit is reset back to the "0" high state the moment output "3" goes high.

Outputs "0" to "2" each drive a relay via an emitter follower transistor, and each relay has a make contact which operates one or more lights. Of course, only one relay will be switched on at a time, and they are switched on sequentially, giving the required moving lights effect. The use of relays to control the lights might seem to be a little old fashioned, but is has the advantage of simplicity. Suitable relays are usually available from surplus components dealers at very low prices, making this method economically attractive. The problem with using triacs in a control circuit of this type is that the circuit would

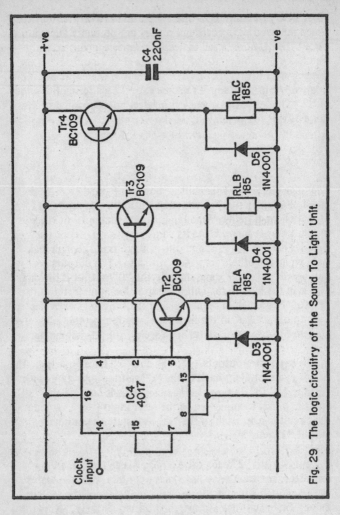

Fig. 29 The logic circuitry of the Sound To Light Unit.

be directly connected to mains supply, unless suitable isolation circuitry was added between the logic outputs and the triac inputs. This would considerably complicate and increase the cost of the project. An alternative would be to use an isolation transformer at the input of the circuit, but is is unlikely that a transformer having suitable characteristics would be obtain-

able. Relays are slower in operation and have shorter operating
lives than solid state devices, but they are perfectly adequate
in both respects as far as this application is concerned.

Mains Circuitry

The circuit diagram of the remainder of the unit is shown in
Figure 30. This shows the mains power supply and lamp
switching circuitry.

The mains supply is coupled to the primary winding of
isolation and step-down transformer, The centre tapped
secondary of T1 is full wave rectified by the push-pull
rectifier which D6 and D7 comprise. C5 smooths the rough
D.C. output from the rectifier. The output voltage is stabilised
at a nominal potential of 12 volts by monolithic voltage
regulator, IC5. C6 and C7 are needed to aid the stability of the
regulator I.C. The regulator has built in current limiting and
thermal shut-down protection circuitry.

The lamps are connected across the switched mains supply, via
the appropriate relay contact. Each relay is shown as controlling three lamps in Figure 30, but each relay can, of course,
control any desired number of lamps, provided the relay
contacts have adequate ratings to handle the chosen number
of lamps.

There should not be too many constructional problems with
this project, but, as with any project which is mains powered
and is controlling mains loads, be very careful when constructing
it. Simple errors can easily result in costly damage and can
even be dangerous. It is probably best for beginners and
inexperienced constructors not to undertake projects of this
type. Note that if the project is housed in a metal case, this
must be connected to the mains earth for reasons of safety. If
a non-metalic case is used, but there is some exposed metal
work (fixing screws etc.) this metal must be properly earthed.
The case must be a type which has a screw-on lid or cover, and
not one having a clip-on type which would permit easy access
to dangerous mains wiring. The output to the lamps can be

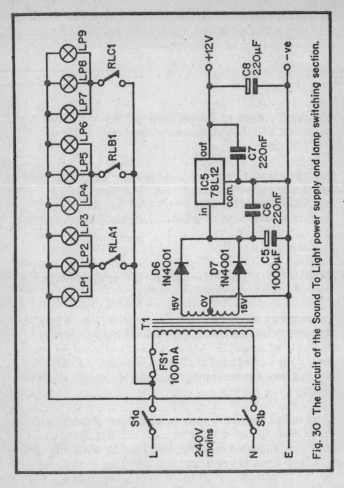

Fig. 30 The circuit of the Sound To Light power supply and lamp switching section.

made by way of a heavy duty terminal block mounted inside the case, or, preferably, via mains outlets mounted on the case.

Remember that IC2, IC3 and IC4 are CMOS devices, and the normal CMOS handling precautions should be taken when dealing with these integrated circuits.

It was not found to be necessary to incorporate interference suppression components on the prototype. If problems with interference are experienced, a 1,000 volt capacitor (or other type capable of operating on the 240V A.C. mains supply) of about 10 nf in value could be added across the switched mains supply, and should adequately reduce the interference.

The lamps can be arranged as shown in Figure 30, and the lights then seem to move in blocks of three. However, there are alternatives, and this is really a matter of the individual experimenting to find the effect which he or she likes best. Although the circuit shows the lamps as being controlled by make contacts, it is possible to use break or changeover contacts in order to obtain other effects. Do make sure though, that the relay contacts are of adequate rating, and if a number of high power lamps are being used, ensure that the mains supply will not be overloaded!

The circuit is designed to take its input from across the loudspeaker output of the amplifier, and it requires an input level of at least a few volts peak to peak. One output terminal of the amplifier must connect to earth, and this must be the one that connects to the earthy input of the sound to light unit. Otherwise the output of the amplifier will be short circuited. It is unlikely that the "AUX" or "TAPE" output of an amplifier will be adequate to drive the unit unless a stage of preamplification is used ahead of the sound to light unit. VR1 is merely adjusted to give the best effect. If it is set at too low a level, the display will operate at or near minimum speed for the amjority of the time. An excessively high setting would merely result in the unit working at or near maximum speed for most of the time. The correct setting will be found somewhere between these two extremes.

Note that when the unit is initially switched on, it is quite possible that one of the unused outputs of IC4 will be the one that assumes the high state. This may result in none of the lamps switching on until the unit cycles through to the condition where the "0" output is high (which could take a few seconds). The unit should then function normally.

Resistors
R1   82k
R2   1.8k
R3   47k
R4   4.7k
R5   1.2k
R6   8.2k
VR1   100k 1og. carbon

Capacitors
C1   1 μF 25V
C2   100 nF plastic foil
C3   10 μF 25V
C4   220 nF plastic foil
C5   1000 μF 40V
C6   220 nF plastic foil
C7   220 nF plastic foil
C8   220 μF 25V

Semiconductors
IC1   555
IC2 to IC4   4017 (3 off)
IC5   78L12 (12 volt 100 mA. positive voltage regulator)
Tr1 to Tr4   BC109 (4 off)
D1   1N4148
D2   1N4148
D3 to D7   1N4001 (5 off)

Switch
S1   D.P.S.T. mains type

Fuse
FS1   100 mA quick blow, 20 mm., and panel mounting
      fuseholder to suit.

Transformer
T1   Standard mains primary, 15V — 0V — 15V secondary
      rated at 100 mA or more (or twin secondaries connected
      in series)

Relays
RLA to RLC   Coil resistance of 185 ohms or more and
operating voltage of 6/12 volts. Contacts of
suitable type and adequate rating for intended
loads and lighting arrangement

Lamps
Mains lamps of required wattage and colours.

Miscellaneous
Case having screw-on cover or lid, mains lead, circuit board,
connecting cables, wire, sockets, etc.

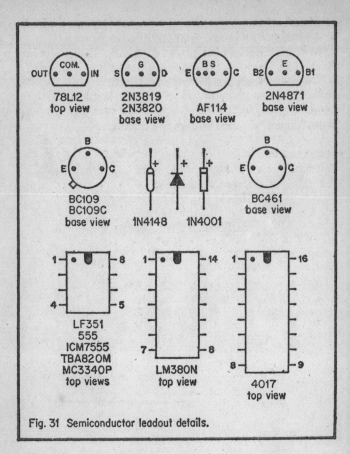

Fig. 31 Semiconductor leadout details.

Please note overleaf is a list of other titles that are available in our range of Radio and Electronics Books.

These should be available from all good Booksellers, Radio Component Dealers and Mail Order Companies.

However, should you experience difficulty in obtaining any title in your area, then please write directly to the publisher enclosing payment to cover the cost of the book plus adequate postage.

If you would like a catalogue of our complete range of Radio and Electronics Books, then please send a Stamped Addressed Envelope to:—

BERNARD BABANI (publishing) LTD
THE GRAMPIANS
SHEPHERDS BUSH ROAD
LONDON W6 7NF
ENGLAND